CPC EXAM STUDY GUIDE

300 PRACTICE QUESTIONS & ANSWERS

Copyright 2020 – All rights reserved
Printed in the United States of America
ISBN 978-1-950159-52-9

No part of this book may be copied, reproduced, or replicated in any manner whether physically or electronically, without first receiving express written permission by the publisher beforehand. All rights reserved.

This book is for general informational purposes. This content is unofficial, privately created, and originally written without any oversight, review, or approval by any such third party. The publishers of this book claim no sponsorship, endorsement, or partnership of any kind with any third party. Specifically, this book and its publishers are not sponsored or affiliated with the AAPC® (a registered trademark of the AAPC).

Every effort has been made to create realistic and accurate information to assist the reader, but no guarantees are made as to that accuracy as any third party may change, modify, or delete any information referenced in this book at any time without notice.

This book is not a replacement or alternative for any coding standards or reference book. This book is designed such that it cannot be used without purchasing the necessary official coding books, some options are listed below for your convenience:

- "CPT Professional 2020": ISBN 978-1622028986, published by the AMA
- "ICD-10-CM 2020": ISBN 978-1622029235, published by the AMA
- "HCPCS 2020 Level II": ISBN 978-1622029303, published by the AMA
- "2020 HCPCS Level II Expert": 978-1626887541, published by the AAPC

Any reference to any codes (CPT, etc.) in this book is for educational purposes and is applied within the standards of fair-use, with all references used only to the extent necessary in the context of preparing for a separate licensing exam and not as an end-use product or software. Please refer to AMA's notice of: 'CPT Copyright 2017 American Medical Association. All rights reserved. CPT® is a registered trademark of the American Medical Association.' The publishers of this book claim no affiliation, endorsement, or sponsorship by the AMA.

Introduction

If you are using this book, you are obviously well on the way to preparing for the big day...
The "big day" of course is when you pass the CPC Exam with flying colors!

We won't bog you down with a bunch of supposed "secrets" like some of "the other guys". The fact is that just like anything else in life, there are no shortcuts and the key to success on the CPC is to practice, practice, and practice. We take that seriously but add that it must be *quality* practice. You've got that here.

You know how the test is formatted, you know what is expected, we won't waste your time rehashing it there. You bought a book of 300 practice questions, not a beginner's guide with a bunch of fluff and filler. There are 2 full length, 150 question tests. Each is divided up by section for easy reference to find answers when you complete each test.

Ideally, you'll treat this like the real test. That means you only use the approved coding reference books (CPT, ICD-10, and HCPCS) and no online resources or smart-phone Apps, and you must limit yourself to the time allowed on test day of 5 hours and 40 minutes.

With that, we won't waste any time....let's get started! You are two practice tests away from your professional certification!

Table of Contents

PRACTICE TEST #1 8
10,000 Series 8
20,000 Series 11
30,000 Series 14
40,000 Series 17
50,000 Series 20
60,000 Series 23
Evaluation and Management 26
Anesthesia 29
Radiology 31
Laboratory / Pathology 34
Medicine 37
Medical Terminology 40
Anatomy 42
ICD-10 CM Diagnosis 44
HCPCS Level II 47
Coding Guidelines 49
Compliance and Regulatory 51

PRACTICE TEST #1 – ANSWER KEY 54
Answer Key - 10,000 Series 54
Answer Key - 20,000 Series 56
Answer Key - 50,000 Series 61
Answer Key - 60,000 Series 63
Answer Key - Evaluation and Management 65
Answer Key - Anesthesia 67
Answer Key - Radiology 68
Answer Key - Laboratory / Pathology 69
Answer Key - Medicine 71
Answer Key - Medical Terminology 72
Answer Key - Anatomy 73
Answer Key - ICD-10 CM Diagnosis 74

Answer Key - HCPCS Level II	75
Answer Key - Coding Guidelines	76
Answer Key - Compliance and Regulatory	77
PRACTICE TEST #2	**78**
10,000 Series	78
20,000 Series	81
30,000 Series	84
40,000 Series	88
50,000 Series	92
60,000 Series	97
Evaluation and Management	102
Anesthesia	106
Radiology	108
Laboratory/Pathology	113
Medicine	115
Medical Terminology	118
Anatomy	120
ICD-10-CM/Diagnosis	122
HCPCS Level II	126
Coding guidelines	128
Compliance and Regulatory	129
ANSWER KEY - PRACTICE TEST #2	**130**
10,000 Series	130
20,000 Series	132
30,000 Series	134
40,000 Series	136
50,000 Series	138
60,000 Series	140
Evaluation and Management	142
Anesthesia	144
Radiology	145
Laboratory/Pathology	147
Medicine	149

Medical Terminology	151
Anatomy	153
ICD-10-CM/Diagnosis	155
HCPCS Level II	157
Coding guidelines	158
Compliance and Regulatory	159

PRACTICE TEST #1
10,000 Series

1. A patient had a benign tumor on the abdomen which was excised and to close the wound, the Dermatologist used the split-thickness skin graft from both thighs, measuring 40 × 20 cm?
   a. 15120 × 8
   b. 15120, 15101 × 7
   c. 15100, 15101 × 7
   d. 15100, 15121 × 7

2. A 68 year old male visited a Dermatologist to consult for the Cyst present on his forehead. The Dermatologist used a 25 gauge needle and a syringe and passed this into the cyst and aspirated the fluid from it and sent the aspirate to the lab for analysis.
   a. 10021
   b. 10022
   c. 19000
   d. 10160

3. A 24 year old lady visited the Dermatologist to consult for her scars over her left cheek(2), right cheek(1) and chin(1). The Dermatologist explained multiple options for the removal of scar and the patient decided to go for abrasion of the scar in the same sitting.
   a. 15786
   b. 15786 x 4
   c. 15780
   d. 15786, 15787 x 3

4. The Dermatologist used Laser surgery to destroy the Squamous Cell Carcinoma (SCC) lesion on the genitalia measuring 0.8 cm?
   a. 17270
   b. 17271
   c. 17272
   d. 11621

5. What code should a radiologist use for placing the localization marker chip in the right breast lesion, preoperatively using mammography?
   a. 19281
   b. 19281, 19282
   c. 19283
   d. 19285

6. OPERATIVE PROCEDURE: Excision of lesion from left thigh.

   INDICATIONS FOR SURGERY: The patient has a big lesion on the left thigh.

   FINDINGS AT SURGERY: There was a non-malignant lesion on the left thigh measuring 6 cm.

   OPERATIVE PROCEDURE: With the patient lying supine, the left thigh was prepped and draped in the usual sterile fashion. The skin and underlying tissues were anesthetized with 20 mL of 1.0% lidocaine.

   Through a 6.5 cm vertical skin incision, the lesion was excised. The incision was closed using 2-0 Vicryl for the deep layers and running 2-0 Prolene subcuticular stitch with Steri-Strips for the skin.
   a. 11404, 12032
   b. 11606, 13121
   c. 11406, 13121
   d. 11406, 12032

7. A 27 year old female presents with skin tags on her face(5), neck(7) and upper back(6) and her dermatologist removes all with the help of the blade.
   a. 11710, L91.0
   b. 17111, L91.0, L91.8
   c. 11200, 11201, L91.8
   d. 11200, L91.8

8. A 49 year old female complains of pain in the right breast and her physician found the cyst like structure on palpation and performed percutaneous needle core biopsy.
    a. 19101
    b. 19100
    c. 11100
    d. 11101

9. A 66 year old male patient returns to the dermatologist with his biopsy reports performed last week. Pathology reports confirmed that the patient has basal cell carcinoma on the right cheek. After discussing all the treatment options, the patient decided to go for Mohs surgery. Dermatologist removes the tumor (first stage) and divides it into six blocks for examination. First stage showed positive margins, so he removed a second stage, which he divided into six blocks. On examination, second blocks prove clear of the skin cancer.
    a. 17311, 17315, 17314, 17315
    b. 17313, 17313, 17314, 17314
    c. 17311, 17315, 17312, 17315
    d. 17312, 17314 x 2

20,000 Series

10. Kyphosis is a disorder of which anatomical site?
    a. Leg
    b. Spine
    c. Male genitalia
    d. Female genitalia

11. The orthopedic surgeon performed arthroscopic meniscectomy of medial meniscus and chondroplasty in patello-femoral joint space.
    a. 29881
    b. 29881, 29880
    c. 29880, 29877
    d. 29881, 29877 -59

12. A 52 year old menopause lady fell on the staircase and suffered a fracture of the right femur head. The Orthopedic surgeon performed hemiarthroplasty of Right hip.
    a. 27125
    b. 27236 -RT
    c. 27269
    d. 27284

13. Jack, a 12 year old boy fell from his bicycle and suffered left patella dislocation. He was brought to the Emergency department, where the doctor performed a closed reduction of patellar dislocation.
    a. 27520
    b. 27560
    c. 27562
    d. 27566

14. A 22 year of male was met with a Road-traffic accident and brought to the Emergency department. He suffered Left femur shaft open displaced transverse fracture of type II. He was taken to the operating room and then open reduction of Left femur shaft fracture was done with intramedullary rod.
    a. 27506, S72.322B
    b. 27506, S72.325B
    c. 27507, S72.322B
    d. 27507, S72.325B

15. A 54 year old female slipped over the slope and fell onto an outstretched hand (FOOSH). She suffered Colles fracture of left hand. The surgeon reduced the fracture with manipulation and put a plaster for the next 45 days.
    a. 25600, S52.532B
    b. 25605, S52.532A
    c. 25600, S52.532A
    d. 25605, S52.539A

16. Bankart's Fracture is fracture of what part of the body?
    a. Spine
    b. Shoulder
    c. Hip
    d. Wrist

17. A 78 years old female patient came to the physician office for a therapeutic injection, in her knee joints for bilateral primary osteoarthritis of knee.
    a. 20605-50, M17.0
    b. 20611-50, M17.0
    c. 20611-RT, M17.2
    d. 20605 x2, M17.0

18. The patient is appropriately prepped and anesthetized, the provider makes small incisions in the shoulder area and inserts an arthroscope through one of the incisions. The provider instills saline solution to inflate the area around the shoulder joint to improve field of view. Removes and reinserts the arthroscope through another incision and excises the distal 1/3 portion of the clavicle, including its articular surface, where it is in contact with the joint. The provider then irrigates the area, checks for bleeding, removes any instruments, and closes the incision.
    a. 29824
    b. 23120
    c. 23125
    d. 23140

30,000 Series

19. The Mitral valve is between
    a. The right atrium and right ventricle
    b. The right ventricle and the pulmonary artery
    c. The left atrium and the left ventricle
    d. The left ventricle and the aorta

20. A 55 year old male patient was diagnosed with Large left-sided pleural effusion. The surgeon punctured the pleural space with the needle and aspirated the fluid. The whole procedure was done under CT guidance.
    a. 32400, 77012
    b. 32400, 76942
    c. 32421, 77012
    d. 32440, 77012

21. A 54 year old male patient got injured in a Road-Traffic accident and brought to the Emergency department with multiple fractured ribs, shallow breathing. Patient was complaining of severe chest pain. The Thoraco Cardiovascular surgeon was called immediately and he assessed the patient and performed tube thoracostomy.
    a. 32160
    b. 32442
    c. 32551
    d. 32100

22. An ENT surgeon performed nasal/sinus endoscopy on the patient and he removed the tissue from anterior ethmoid sinus.
    a. 31255
    b. 31237
    c. 31254
    d. 31296

23. A 55 year old male patient underwent CABG procedure. The patient was appropriately prepped and anesthetized, the provider then harvested two vein segments from the saphenous vein in the leg endoscopically. He then made a midline sternotomy and inserted the aortic and venous cannulas to establish cardiopulmonary bypass. He then injected a cardioplegia solution to stop the heart for the procedure. He attached the distal ends of the two prepared saphenous veins to appropriate locations on the sides of the diseased target vessels. He then attached the proximal ends of the grafts to holes punched into the ascending aorta. He then weaned the patient off the bypass pump. The provider then irrigated the area, checked for bleeding, removed any instruments, and closed the incision in layers.
    a. 33511, 33508
    b. 33534, 33508
    c. 33510, 33508
    d. 33533, 33517

24. A 66 year old male patient was admitted to the ICU for pneumonia. The ICU physician performed diagnostic flexible bronchoscopy and he performed bronchial alveolar lavage (BAL) in which he used saline solution to wash the cells from alveoli and then he obtained several biopsies from the trachea, main stem, and/or lobar bronchus through a transbronchial needle aspiration technique.
    a. 31624, 31628
    b. 31622, 31629
    c. 31622, 31629
    d. 31624, 31629

25. The patient presents with nasal polyp. The provider prepped and anesthetized the patient and identified the location of the polyp. The provider chooses the snare technique and passes the loop over the polyp, and pushes the sheath of the snare against the base of the polyp. He then uses the snare, or a scalpel to detach the polyp from its base. He then sutures the defect to close it.
    a. 30110
    b. 30115
    c. 30117
    d. 30118

26. The 58 years old patient presents with throat pain and difficulty in speaking from the last 3-4 days. The physician prepped and anesthetized the patient and inserted a flexible laryngoscope into the nose and viewed the laryngeal and hypopharyngeal structures along with the vocal folds. The provider then uses biopsy forceps to take samples of suspicious areas or lesions. He sends these samples to the laboratory for testing.
    a. 31570
    b. 31577
    c. 31576
    d. 31535

27. Patient had tricuspid valve prolapse, and a tricuspid valve ring was inserted with a cardiopulmonary bypass.
    a. 33468
    b. 33430
    c. 33460
    d. 33465

40,000 Series

28. A 14 year old girl was diagnosed with Adenoiditis. After a successful partial adenoidectomy a few years back, the patient has developed Adenoiditis. The surgeon has decided to perform adenoidectomy. After administration of anesthesia the patient is prepped and draped in a sterile fashion. A mouth gag is inserted and the physician uses an adenoid curette or biting forceps to remove the secondary adenoid lesion. The removal is further confirmed with the use of a laryngeal mirror. Bleeding is then controlled with electrocautery.
    a. 42830
    b. 42831
    c. 42821
    d. 42836

29. A 24 year old male was taken to the ER for severe abdominal pain and vomiting. The general surgeon suspected appendicitis and performed an emergency appendectomy for ruptured appendix.
    a. 44950
    b. 44955
    c. 44960
    d. 44970

30. A 52 year old male patient presents with ulcerative colitis. He was elected for diagnostic colonoscopy for malignancy. The patient was placed in the left lateral decubitus position and after conscious sedation; a lubricated Olympus CF 100 TL video colonoscope was inserted into the rectum and advanced to cecum without difficulty. Multiple biopsies were taken of the right colon. The patient tolerated the procedure well.
    a. 44389
    b. 45380
    c. 45378
    d. 45379

31. A 48 year old male patient presents to the physician office for the concern of a cholelithiasis with acute cholecystitis. The physician performed a percutaneous transhepatic cholangiography with injection procedure. After that he performed a percutaneous transhepatic stent placement under radiological supervision and interpretation.
    a. 47532
    b. 47532, 47538
    c. 47538
    d. 47531, 47538

32. A 38 year old female patient comes to the physician office complaining of severe lower GI bleeding. Physician performed a colonoscopy and learnt to have some stricture around the colonic passage, he then performed dilation of the strictures by using a balloon.
    a. 45303
    b. 45340
    c. 45386
    d. 45382

33. An 67 year old female had been diagnosed with proximal small bowel obstruction. The surgeon decided to examine the abdomen and release the obstructions, so after all consents and explaining associated risk and benefits, she was taken to the operating room, where the surgeon put her on general anesthesia and made an abdominal incision by excising the skin and subcutaneous tissue. After examining, Surgeon found that there were adhesions along the entire length of the small bowel and the small intestine was stuck up to the anterior abdominal wall. The surgeon freed up all the adhesions, which relieved the obstruction.
    a. 44005
    b. 44180
    c. 58740
    d. 58660

34. Which of the following organs is not part of the Digestive system?
    a. Stomach
    b. Colon
    c. Pancreas
    d. Spleen

35. A 48 year old male patient was seen in the outpatient GI lab for rectal pain and bleeding. A colonoscopy was performed which revealed 2 polyps in the descending colon. All 3 polyps were removed using snare technique.
    a. 45382
    b. 45383
    c. 45384
    d. 45385

36. A 68 year old male patient underwent a repair of an initial umbilical hernia. The patient was appropriately prepped and anesthetized, the provider made a small incision over the abdominal region. He then inserted an instrument to inflate the abdomen with CO2. He inserted a scope along with additional ports into small incisions in the peritoneal cavity. The provider then identified the umbilical hernia and removed the adhesions. He then reduced the hernia, maneuvering it to be in proper anatomical position.
    a. 49652
    b. 49560
    c. 49653
    d. 49652, 49568

50,000 Series

37. The Obstetrician performed a Total Abdominal Hysterectomy (TAH) on a 27 year old female, immediately following a C-section due to a ruptured uterus during labor. What codes should be used for these complicated procedures including antepartum and postpartum care?
    a. 59515, 59525
    b. 59510, 59525
    c. 59514, 59135
    d. 59618, 59135

38. A 30 year old female came to her Obs & Gyn provider's office with an ectopic pregnancy. The provider performed a laparoscopic treatment for the ectopic pregnancy and also performed salpingectomy and oophorectomy.
    a. 59150
    b. 59135
    c. 59120
    d. 59151

39. An 42 year old female patient was admitted to the hospital with abnormal vaginal discharge due to rectocele and cystocele. An anteroposterior colporrhaphy was done to repair the defect.
    a. 57260
    b. 57283
    c. 57240, 57250
    d. 57265

40. A 37 year old male presented to the physician with carcinoma in-situ of the testis and warts on his penis. The provider performed cryosurgery to destroy the warts and performed a radical orchiectomy through an inguinal incision.
    a. 54060, 54522
    b. 54056, 54522
    c. 54056, 54530
    d. 54056, 54535

41. A 44 year old male was diagnosed with recurrent transitional cell carcinoma of the bladder. After putting him on general anesthesia, the Urologist passed a 21 French Cystoscope into his bladder. Random biopsies of the bladder were taken. The hyperemic area of the bladder was fulgurated. A total of 0.3 cm of bladder was fulgurated.
    a. 52214
    b. 52224
    c. 52204
    d. 52234

42. A 62 year old female presents to her General physician with renal abscess. The physician introduced a catheter percutaneously into renal pelvis for the drainage of that abscess under radiological supervision and interpretation.
    a. 50392, 74480
    b. 50392, 74475
    c. 50393, 74480
    d. 50393, 74475

43. A 54 year old male patient presents to the Urologist office. The Urologist performed a percutaneous needle biopsy of the prostate under Fluoroscopic guidance.
    a. 55700, 77002
    b. 55706, 77002
    c. 55705, 77002
    d. 55720, 77002

44. A 49 year old female patient presents to the Urologist with a vesicouterine fistula due to endometriosis of the uterus. The Urologist closed the vesicouterine fistula.
    a. 51880
    b. 51900
    c. 51920
    d. 51925

45. Which organ is not considered part of the female reproductive system?
    a. Ureter
    b. Uterus
    c. Ovary
    d. Cervix

46. A 54 year old female patient was diagnosed with ovarian cancer and underwent a Trans-Abdominal removal of uterus, bilateral fallopian tubes and ovaries.
    a. 58200
    b. 58953
    c. 58150
    d. 58541

47. A 75 year old male was diagnosed with BPH with obstruction. Patient decided to go for TURP. During a transurethral resection of the prostate (TURP), the surgeon inserted a resectoscope via the urethra and removed a significant portion of the prostate.
    a. 52630
    b. 52601
    c. 52647
    d. 53852

48. A 56 year old male patient underwent kidney stone destruction through shock waves. The patient was placed on a special table with a fluid-filled cushion placed against his body. The physician used fluoroscopic imaging guidance to locate the calculus. Then the physician aimed ultrasound shock waves at the stone through the water medium, breaking up the calculus into small fragments that can pass easily through the urinary tract.
    a. 50590
    b. 52317
    c. 50081
    d. 52317

60,000 Series

49. The Ophthalmologist performed removal of lens material for cataracts using a pars plana approach with a vitrectomy.
    a. 66840
    b. 66850
    c. 66852
    d. 66920

50. A 39 year old male patient was diagnosed with recurrent herniated disk at L4-L5 on the left side. The Spinal surgeon performed a repeated laminotomy and foraminotomy at the L4-L5 single interspace.
    a. 63042
    b. 63042, 63044
    c. 63047
    d. 63056

51. A 52 year old female underwent a vertebral corpectomy of 2 lumbar vertebra through transperitoneal approach.
    a. 63090
    b. 63090, 63091
    c. 63087, 63088
    d. 63087

52. A 38 year old female patient underwent a tympanoplasty with mastoidotomy along with ossicular chain reconstruction.
    a. 69636
    b. 69635
    c. 69637
    d. 69632

53. A 32 year old female patient admitted with thyroid and parathyroid glands enlargement. The surgeon performed a left total thyroid lobectomy with isthmusectomy.
    a. 60212
    b. 60220
    c. 60225
    d. 60240

54. A 11 year old kid presented to the ER department complaining of ear pain. The doctor on duty examined the patient and performed Removal of foreign body from the external auditory canal without general anesthesia.
    a. 69200
    b. 69205
    c. 69210
    d. 69220

55. A 54 year old male patient had an injury to the left plantar nerve. It later developed into Morton's neuroma. The Podiatrist performed an excision of the neuroma.
    a. 28086
    b. 28088
    c. 28080
    d. 64774

56. A 28 year of male patient arrived at the Emergency department with repetitive hiccoughs. The doctor on duty injected a single bolus of procaine solution in the phrenic nerve.
    a. 64746
    b. 49041
    c. 64412
    d. 64410

57. Which endocrine glands sit atop of kidneys:
    a. Thyroid
    b. Adrenal
    c. Pituitary
    d. Hypothalamus

58. The 66 year old male patient was appropriately prepped and anesthetized. The Ophthalmologist makes a small incision in the eye and then enters the capsule and removes the hard nucleus from the lens of the eye. He used an iris expansion device to dilate the eye. He then evacuates the soft lens cortex, leaving the capsule partially intact. He inserts a prosthetic intraocular lens after irrigation and aspiration. He finally sutures the cut and infuses antibiotic solution into the eye.
    a. 66982
    b. 66983
    c. 66984
    d. 66985

59. A 12 year old school going boy came into the Emergency room with high fever and headache for the past 4 days. A lumbar puncture was performed and spinal fluid was sent to the lab to rule out the Encephalitis or Meningitis.
    a. 20605
    b. 62272
    c. 62270
    d. 62268

60. A patient has spinal stenosis located between L4–L5 disc space. Surgeon performed a laminectomy on L4 by removing the spinous process and lamina of L4. Surgeon also performed decompression at the L4–L5 level.
    a. 63047
    b. 63005
    c. 63017
    d. 63030

Evaluation and Management

61. Mr. Adams is a 69 year old medicare patient. He was presented to his Primary care Physician for his routine Annual physical exam. During the examination the PCP noticed a suspicious wart on Mr. Adams's neck. The PCP completed the annual exam and documented the Detailed history and exam. The PCP also discussed counsel Mr. Adams to quit smoking. The PCP then turned his attention to the mole and did a complete work up. He documented a comprehensive history and examination and medical decision making of moderate complexity. He also referred Mr. Adams to a local Dermatologist for an evaluation and biopsy.
    a. G0439, 99212-25
    b. G0439, 99215-25
    c. G0402, 99205-25
    d. G0402, 99215-25

62. A 62 year old established male patient presents to his PCP office for a routine preventive checkup. The physician conducted a multi-system history and physical examination and the checkup took a total of 45 minutes of face-to-face time with the PCP.
    a. 99214, Z00.5
    b. 99403, Z00.6
    c. 99386, Z00.00
    d. 99396, Z00.00

63. The proper way to code the 94 minutes of critical care services is:
    a. 99291
    b. 99291, 99291x2
    c. 99291, 99175
    d. 99291, 99292

64. A 38 year old female patient presented to the ER department with Abdominal pain. The doctor on duty rendered a comprehensive history, detailed exam and moderate complexity MDM in the emergency department setting.
    a. 99284
    b. 99283
    c. 99285
    d. 99282

65. A 44 year old male patient was on observation status for 10 hours to assess the outcome of a fall at the construction site. The physician discharged the patient on the same day considering no need for further observation. The physician provided a detailed history and examination and MDM of low complexity.
    a. 99218
    b. 99235
    c. 99234
    d. 99238

66. A Cardiologist admitted a 55 year old male patient to the Acute care hospital with Chest Pain. The physician completed a comprehensive history and physical examination. The physician ordered an electrocardiogram, x-rays, and routine laboratory workup. The physician considered the probable diagnoses of pericarditis, Gastritis, Angina pectoris, unstable angina, dissecting aneurysm or pulmonary infarction indicating a high level of medical decision making complexity.
    a. 99236
    b. 99223
    c. 99245
    d. 99222

67. A 54 year old diabetic patient comes to the physician's office for his routine blood sugar check. His blood is drawn by the Registered Nurse Practitioner.
    a. 99215
    b. 99211
    c. 99241
    d. 99201

68. A 57 year old male patient was referred by his Family physician to a Cardiologist to rule out the reason for Tachycardia. The Cardiologist examined the patient and sent his recommendations and a written report back to his family physician. Which category or subcategory of evaluation and management codes would you select for Cardiologist Visit.
    a. Office visit, new patient
    b. Office visit, established patient
    c. Outpatient consultation
    d. Preventive evaluation services

69. A 11 month old male infant was brought to the Emergency room with high fever and trouble breathing. The physician provided Critical Care for stabilizing the patient.
    a. 99291
    b. 99291
    c. 99471
    d. 99472

Anesthesia

70. A toddler of 16 months old has to undergo Ventral Hernia repair. What should be the anesthesia code?
    a. 00820
    b. 00830
    c. 00832
    d. 00834

71. A male patient of age 71 year has severe asthma from the last 10 years. He has been given anesthesia for a procedure of a tendon in his upper arm.
    a. 01714-P4
    b. 01714-P3, 99100
    c. 01712-P4, 99100
    d. 01716-P3

72. A 5 year old boy has gone for tympanotomy from his left ear under general anesthesia.
    a. 00170-P2
    b. 00120-P1
    c. 00126-P1
    d. 00124-P2

73. A healthy patient of age 76 years had undergone a hip dislocation following a fall. He has been placed under GA before hip reduction procedure. The patient was prepared at 10:00 AM in the morning and at 10:15 AM the anesthesiologist induced him with anesthesia. Anesthesiologist is monitoring the patient's vitals, capnography, etc throughout the procedure. At 10:30 surgeon begins his procedure and completes that at 11:00 AM. The anesthesiologist is still monitoring the patient. At 11:15 AM, he released the patient to nurse for Post-operative supervision. At 11:30 AM the patient is fully alert and taken to recovery. What would be the total duration, the Anesthesiologist should charge for anesthesia?
    a. 1 hour
    b. 1 hour and 15 minutes
    c. 45 minutes
    d. 30 minutes

74. A 44 year old male patient underwent coronary artery bypass grafting (CABG) and Anesthesia was provided for the procedure along with the oxygenator pump.
    Report the code(s) for Anesthesia procedure.
    a. 00567
    b. 00561
    c. 00580
    d. 00562

75. The 24 year old pregnant woman had a cesarean delivery and general anesthesia was provided for the procedure.
    a. 01960
    b. 01964
    c. 01962
    d. 01961

Radiology

76. Appropriate code for a Magnetic Resonance Imaging of the lumbar spine without contrast, then followed by with contrast and further sequence.
    a. 72148, 72149
    b. 72149
    c. 72158
    d. 72148

77. A 44 year old male met with the car accident and suffered Bilateral Knee joint effusion. The physician performed an arthrogram in the hospital. The physician also performed the injection procedure.
    a. 27370, 73580 -50
    b. 27370 -50, 73580 -50
    c. 27370 -50, 73580
    d. 27370, 73580

78. The oncologist administers radiopharmaceuticals prior to localization of inflammatory processes using SPECT.
    a. 78803
    b. 78807
    c. 78802
    d. 78808

79. A 62 year old male patient is brought to the radiology department suffering from severe abdominal pain, vomiting and problems swallowing. The provider ordered a UGI and a barium enema to diagnose the problem. During the exam, the radiologist also has films of his finding taken by the hospital's radiologic technician.
    a. 74240, 74270
    b. 74245, 74280
    c. 74240, 74280
    d. 74245, 74270

80. A 1 year old child is brought into the emergency department as he swallows a penny. The ED physician orders a foreign body localization films on the child to locate the penny. After careful examination, it is located in the stomach.
    a. 76001
    b. 76010
    c. 74020
    d. 74022

81. What would be the correct CPT code(s) for percutaneous radiofrequency ablation of one or more liver tumors under ultrasonic guidance?
    a. 47380, 76940
    b. 47382, 76940
    c. 47382, 76942
    d. 47380, 76942

82. CT scan of lungs was done without contrast. What is the CPT code for it?
    a. 71260
    b. 71270
    c. 71250
    d. 75572

83. A 52 year old female complains of pain in her right breast and she can feel some tightness in both the breasts. To rule out etiology, the provider performs a mammography by placing each of the patient's breasts between two plates and presses the plates together firmly. The compressor has an X-ray plate that exposes the breast to radiation to obtain images. To enhance detection of any abnormalities and improve the analysis, the provider uses computer-aided detection software to further analyze the images.
    a. 77066
    b. 77065
    c. 77067
    d. 77053

84. A 62 year old male patient patient is receiving brachytherapy for his prostate cancer. Seven radioactive seeds were interstitially placed within the prostate.
    a. 77762
    b. 77761
    c. 77763
    d. 77770

Laboratory / Pathology

85. A 56 year old male patient was presented to his PCP's office with complaints of abdominal pain and episodes of blood in his stool. The PCP performed a digital rectal exam and tests for occult blood. Dr. Smith documents this blood occult test was done for purposes other than colorectal cancer screening. How would you report the occult blood test?
    a. 82270
    b. 82271
    c. 82272
    d. 82274

86. A 48 year old female patient was having intermittent abdominal pain, bloating and diarrhea. Her symptoms have worsened over the past couple of weeks. Her physician ordered a fecal Calprotectin test to check for Crohn's disease.
    a. 83993
    b. 82270
    c. 82272
    d. 82274

87. Physician ordered a comprehensive metabolic panel (CMP) test and also wanted blood work on calcium ions.
    a. 80047
    b. 80053, 80047
    c. 80053, 82330
    d. 82330

88. A pathologist performs a comprehensive consultation and report after reviewing a patient's records and specimens from another facility.
    a. 88329
    b. 80502
    c. 88329
    d. 99244

89. A 43 year old male patient had following lab tests:
    Calcium ionized, Carbon dioxide, Chloride, Creatinine, Glucose, Potassium, Sodium, Urea Nitrogen (BUN)
    a. 80048
    b. 80053
    c. 82330, 82374, 82435, 82565, 82947, 84132, 84295, 84520
    d. 80047

90. A 48 year old female patient is having borderline diabetic. Her PCP sent her to the laboratory for having an oral glucose tolerance test done. She drank the glucose and 3 blood specimens were taken every 30 to 60 minutes up to 2 hours to determine how quickly the glucose gets cleared from the blood.
    a. 82947 x 5
    b. 82951
    c. 80422
    d. 82946

91. A 35 year old female patient undergoing breast augmentation surgery and already on Coumadin. Before scheduling the surgery, the provider tested her for a PT test. What CPT code describes this test?
    a. 85002
    b. 85347
    c. 85610
    d. 85670

92. A 32 year old female patient was tested with following tests: total Calcium, Carbon dioxide (bicarbonate), Chloride, Creatinine, Glucose, Potassium, Sodium, Urea nitrogen and Ammonia. What is/are the correct code(s)?
    a. 80047
    b. 80048
    c. 80047, 82140
    d. 80053

93. A 32 year old male died of a gunshot injury in a police encounter. An autopsy was performed to collect the evidence required for further investigation and lawsuit trials. What code(s) describes this procedure?
    a. 88020
    b. 88037
    c. 88040
    d. 88099

Medicine

94. A 43 year old patient presented to the Physical Therapy office with a problem of hyperhidrosis. The Physical Therapist evaluated the patient and decided to do Iontophoresis. The provider applied electric current by placing the hands in water and then passed electricity through the water, gradually increasing the current. The PT provided this treatment for 15 minute.
    a. 97032
    b. 97034
    c. 97033
    d. 97014

95. An adult of 22 years of age was presented to ER post dog-bite. The doctor on cleaned the wound and applied dressing. The doctor also administered the Rabies immune globulin, human injection, IM.
    a. 90375
    b. 90376
    c. 90460
    d. 90466

96. Molly, a 28 year old female professional cyclathon player has suffered from dehydration after the competition. She was taken into the primary care doctor's office. The PCP checked Molly and ordered hydration therapy with normal saline. The hydration lasted 50 minutes.
    a. 96360, 96361
    b. 96360
    c. 96361
    d. 96374

97. A 55 year old male patient underwent a percutaneous transluminal coronary atherectomy (PTCA) with a balloon to the left main coronary artery. During the same session the surgeon placed three drug coated stents in the left circumflex artery (LC).
    a. 92924, 92933
    b. 92933
    c. 92924, 92925
    d. 92933, 92934

98. A 54 year old Cancer patient came for Chemotherapy infusion. The oncologist noted that the patient was in a dehydration state, so he decided to first administer a hydration infusion. The infusion lasted for 1 hour and 28 minutes.
    a. 96360
    b. 96360, 96361
    c. 96422, 96423
    d. 96422

99. A 35 year old male patient came to the Psychiatrist with Bipolar disorder. The psychiatrist provided psychotherapy for 30 minutes.
    a. 90839
    b. 90846
    c. 90832, 90833
    d. 90832

100. A 68 year old patient with Diabetic Mellitus visited his Primary Care Physician for a scheduled Flu shot.
    a. 90667, 90471
    b. 90672, 90473
    c. 90647, 90471
    d. 90667, 90472

101. A 26 year old female patient has come to Allergist with severe allergic reactions. The patient has known allergy for eggs. An Allergist prepares 3 vials of single dose antigens and injects in the patient to rule out if the patient has accidentally eaten the egg or egg based products.
    a. 95130
    b. 95144 x 3 units
    c. 95145 x 3 units
    d. 95134

102. A 28 year female patient has Iron Deficiency Anemia. Gastroenterologist has decided to do Capsule endoscopy to rule out the obscure GI bleeding.

    The Gastroenterologist gave the patient an activated endoscopic capsule to swallow with normal water. As the capsule passed through the digestive tract, it automatically took images of the gastrointestinal lumen. The Gastroenterologist then transferred the data from the image recording device to the computer. He then analyzed and interpreted the recorded data and prepared a written report.

    a. 91020
    b. 91110 f
    c. 91010
    d. 91111

Medical Terminology

103. Chondroblastoma of the proximal humerus also referred as?
    a. Brenor's tumor
    b. Codman's Tumor
    c. Pancaostal Tumor
    d. Warthin Tumor

104. Pulmonary veins carry oxygenated blood from lungs to the left atrium of the heart?
    a. True
    b. False

105. Angiography is the study of?
    a. Brain
    b. Blood Vessels
    c. Heart
    d. Adrenal Gland

106. Rheumatologist is described by which of the following statements?
    a. A specialist who provides treatment to women during pregnancy, childbirth, and their aftercare
    b. A specialist who provides the diagnosis and surgical treatment of bone disorders
    c. A specialist who provides the diagnosis and treatment of musculoskeletal disease and systemic autoimmune conditions
    d. A specialist who provides medical care and drug treatments focused on mental and cognitive disorders

107. A Myringotomy is a surgical incision on which part of the human body?
    a. Eyelid
    b. Nasal Sinus
    c. Ear Drum
    d. Penis

108. In clinical terminology, what does ERG stand for?
    a. Emergency Response Guidebook
    b. Electroretinography
    c. Electrorenography
    d. Electrorhidogram

109. What part of the human body, does onychomycosis refer to?
    a. Ovary
    b. Testes
    c. Nail
    d. Hair

110. Which procedure defines Thoracostomy?
    a. Surgical procedure to gain access into the pleural space of the chest
    b. Small incision of the chest wall, with maintenance of the opening for drainage
    c. Procedure to examine the pleural lining of the lungs and the surface of the lungs through scope
    d. Surgical procedure to permanently collapse tuberculous cavities by resection of ribs from the chest wall

111. "Arthron" is a Greek word, which refers to:
    a. Bone
    b. Ligament
    c. Joint
    d. Cartilage

Anatomy

112. Choroid coat is found in which body part of the human body?
    a. Eye
    b. Spinal canal
    c. Brain stem
    d. Femur bone

113. A malignant bone tumor is described by which term ?
    a. Myeloid Melanoma
    b. Chondrosarcoma
    c. Lymphoma
    d. Osteosarcoma

114. With respect to Ear Bone, identify the one which is not related.
    a. Stapes
    b. malleus
    c. Hamate
    d. Incus

115. Which term is best fit for the lower third of the small intestine?
    a. Tenue
    b. Ileum
    c. jejunum
    d. Duodenum

116. What type of graft is Xenograft?
    a. A tissue graft from a donor of the same species
    b. A tissue graft from one species to an unlike species
    c. A tissue graft from one point to another of the same individual's body.
    d. Tissue or organ transplanted from one member of a species to another, genetically identical member of the species

117. Which nerve controls the motor function of adductor longus muscle? is the obturator nerve found?
    a. Sciatic Nerve
    b. Obturator Nerve
    c. Radial Nerve
    d. Femoral Nerve

118. How many valves does the Human Heart have?
    a. 4
    b. 2
    c. 3
    d. 1

119. Caecum is considered part of:
    a. Large Intestine
    b. Small intestine
    c. Liver
    d. Kidney

120. Where is the Prostate gland found?
    a. On bottom of the hypothalamus at the base of the brain
    b. On the front of the neck
    c. Between the bladder and the penis
    d. In the peritoneal cavity

ICD-10 CM Diagnosis

121. A 28 year old male patient received counselling on Tobacco abuse.
    a. Z71.6
    b. Z71.9
    c. Z71.89
    d. Z72.0

122. A 52 year old male patient was diagnosed with COVID-19 and he has shortness of breath and cough.
    a. U07.1
    b. U07.1, R05
    c. U07.1, R05, R06.0
    d. U07.1, Z20.8

123. A 28 year old female patient was brought to Emergency with a left hand injury. X-Ray revealed a spiral fracture of the shaft of humerus.
    a. S42.325A
    b. S42.322A
    c. S42.302A
    d. S42.323A

124. A bus driver got injured in collision with another bus in a traffic accident. He was brought to the ER department with chest pain.
    a. R07.9, V74.5XXD
    b. R07.9, V74.5XXA
    c. R07.89, V74.1XXA
    d. R07.89, V74.0XXA

125. A 53 year old male patient has uncontrolled diabetes and still on Insulin. He also has a personal history of long-term insulin use.
    a. E10.9
    b. Z79.4
    c. E11.8
    d. E11.65

126. A 44 year old female had her carbuncle removed from the groin region. Pathology report indicated staphylococcal infection.
    a. L02.234, B95.61
    b. L02.235, B95.61
    c. L02.234, B95.8
    d. L02.235, B95.8

127. Fracture of right Tibia due to osteogenesis imperfecta:
    a. M84.661A, Q78.0
    b. M84.663A, Q78.0
    c. M84.669A, Q78.0
    d. M84.662A, Q78.0

128. Viral meningitis due to AIDS:
    a. A87.8
    b. B20, A87.8
    c. B33.8, A87.8
    d. B20

129. A 60 year old Diabetic patient came to the Physician office to rule out the COVID-19 infection. He has travelled abroad with his friend 1 week back and now his friend came positive for COVID-19 infection. Report the correct ICD-10 CM code for this visit.
    a. Z20.828
    b. Z03.818
    c. Z03.810
    d. Z20.821

130. A 48 year old female patient with Malignant cancer of right Breast, visited her oncologist to receive an injection of retacrit. Patient has developed anemia post chemotherapy treatment.
    a. D64.81, C50.911
    b. D64.2, C50.911
    c. D64.81
    d. C50.911, D64.81

131. A 34 year old male patient visited the General Physician for his routine follow-up of Diabetes Mellitus. Patient has no complications and Diabetes Mellitus is well controlled as the patient is on oral hypoglycemics.
    a. E11.9 XX
    b. E11.8
    c. E09.9
    d. E10.9

132. A 54 year old female patient has a carbuncle on her left thigh. The Dermatologist performed incision and drainage. What ICD-10 CM code can be reported?
    a. L02.435
    b. L02.436 xx
    c. L02.425
    d. L02.426

HCPCS Level II

133. What modifier is used for the upper left eyelid?
    a. E1
    b. E2
    c. E3
    d. E4

134. A patient with Colorectal cancer was injecting Fluorouracil as part of his chemotherapy regimen. He receives 500 mg once a week through intravenous infusion.
    a. J9100
    b. J9070
    c. J3490
    d. J9190

135. A patient with diabetes is fitted for custom molded shoes. What is the HCPCS codes and code range for such shoe fitting?
    a. A5500-A5513
    b. K0001-K0899
    c. L3201-L3649
    d. E0100-E8002

136. A 340lbs paraplegic patient needs a special sized wheelchair with fixed armrests and elevating leg rests.
    a. E1195
    b. E1160
    c. E1222
    d. E1224

137. Which set of HCPCS Level II codes would be utilized to report Pathology and Laboratory Services?
    a. Q codes
    b. J codes
    c. S codes
    d. P codes

138. What HCPCS Level II Modifier would be used to identify Right Thumb?
    a. FA
    b. F6
    c. F5
    d. F9

Coding Guidelines

139. Coinsurance is defined as the percentage of costs of a covered health care service you pay after you've paid your deductible.
    a. True
    b. False

140. Category III codes are temporary codes for emerging technology, services, and procedures. If a category III code exists for any procedure/service, then it should be used, then using the Unlisted procedure/service from CPT I code categories.
    a. True
    b. False

141. CPT codes's copyright is held by?
    a. World Health Organization (WHO)
    b. Centers for Medicare & Medicaid Services (CMS)
    c. American Medical Association (AMA)
    d. United States Department of Health and Human Services (DHHS)

142. What does CM stand for in ICD-10 CM codes?
    a. Content Management
    b. Clinical Master
    c. Clinical Modification
    d. Clinical Medical

143. A 70 year old Medicare patient was referred to a Cardiologist for consultation service. What code category can a Cardiologist bill for Consultation services for Medicare patients?
    a. New patient E/M Codes (99201 - 99205)
    b. Established patient E/M Codes (99211 - 99215)
    c. Office Consultation E/M Codes (99241 - 99245)
    d. Inpatient Consultation E/M Codes (99251 - 99255)

144. Which statement is true for Exclude1 in ICD-10 CM coding?
    a. Excludes1 is used when two conditions cannot occur together
    b. Excludes1 is used when two conditions can be reported if they exist together.

Compliance and Regulatory

145. What does Medical necessity mean with respect to Medical coding and billing?
    a. Without treatment the patient will suffer permanent disability or death
    b. The service requires medical treatment
    c. The condition of the patient justifies the service provided
    d. The care provided met quality standards

146. Which of the following statements is true regarding Medicare Part B?
    a. It helps cover home health care charges
    b. It helps cover SNF charges
    c. It helps cover hospice charges
    d. It helps cover outpatient charges

147. Which form do Physicians use to bill for their professional services?
    a. UB-04
    b. HCFA-1500
    c. CMS-1450
    d. Ub-92

148. Which place of service code should be reported on the physician's claim for a surgical procedure performed in an outpatient setting of the hospital facility?
    a. 21
    b. 22
    c. 24
    d. 11

149. What is the full-form of HIPAA?
    a. Health information Portability and Accountability Act
    b. Health Insurance Portability and Accountability Act
    c. Health information of Patient and Accountability Act
    d. Health Insurance Portability and Advisory Act

150. What is considered PHI under HIPAA?
    a. Medical Record Numbers
    b. Social Security Numbers
    c. Name
    d. Employment Status

PRACTICE TEST #1 – ANSWER KEY
Answer Key - 10,000 Series

1. **Answer: C**

   CPT 15100 represents Split-thickness autograft, trunk, arms, legs; first 100 sq cm or less. It is the correct code for Abdomen and Thigh split-thickness graft for the first 100 cm2. For each additional 100 cm2, use multiple units of Add-on code +CPT 15101.

2. **Answer: A**

   Correct answer is A, as the Dermatologist did the FNA and didn't use any image guidance for the procedure.

3. **Answer: D**

   Correct answer is D, as the Dermatologist performed Abrasion of the scars. Use CPT code 15876 for first scar/lesion and use multiple units of add-on +15787 for each additional scar/lesion abrasion upto 4 lesions.

4. **Answer: B**

   Correct answer is option B, as the Dermatologist used Laser surgery to destroy the malignant lesion from genitalia.

5. **Answer: A**

   Correct code is CPT 19281 as it represents "Placement of breast localization device(s) (eg, clip, metallic pellet, wire/needle, radioactive seeds), percutaneous; first lesion, including mammographic guidance"

6. **Answer: D**

   CPT 11406 represents the excision of a benign lesion more than 4 cm. The repair is of intermediate type so CPT code 12032 should be used.

7. **Answer: C**

   CPT code 11200 should be used for removal of skin tags, any area up to and including 15 lesions. For additional skin tag removal, use +11201 code for upto 10 additional skin tags of any area. ICD-10 code L91.8 is the correct code for skin tags.

8. **Answer: B**

   CPT code 19100 should be used, when the provider removes a core tissue sample from a breast lesion to diagnose conditions such as breast cancer.

9. **Answer: C**

Report CPT code 17311 for first stage Mohs Surgery from the face, upto 5 tissue blocks and for any additional blocks use CPT + 17315. For the second stage Mohs surgery from the face, upto 5 tissue blocks, use CPT +17312.

Answer Key - 20,000 Series

10. Answer: B

Kyphosis is a spinal disorder in which an excessive outward curve of the spine results in an abnormal rounding of the upper back.

11. Answer: D

CPT 29881 for arthroscopic medial meniscectomy. CPT 29877 should be billed separately with modifier -59 as the chondroplasty was done in a separate compartment of the knee joint.

12. Answer: B

CPT code 27125 is reported for degenerative changes, not fracture conditions. CPT code 27236 (open treatment of femoral fracture, proximal end, neck, internal fixation or prosthetic replacement) would be used to report a hemiarthroplasty for a hip fracture.

13. Answer: B

CPT 27560 represents "Closed treatment of patellar dislocation; without anesthesia". If it's nowhere mentioned that anesthesia was used, so use the CPT code without anesthesia, if present.

14. Answer: A

Correct codes for ORIF with intramedullary rod for Left Femur shaft type II displaced transverse fracture are CPT 27506 and ICD-10 CM S72.322B.

15. Answer: B

Correct ICD-10 CM code for Colles' fracture of left radius is S52.532A. The correct CPT code for Closed reduction of Colles' fracture is 25605.

16. Answer: B

Bankart's Fracture is defined as fracture of anterior glenoid associated with anterior shoulder dislocation.

17. Answer: B

CPT code 20611 is for an arthrocentesis, aspiration and/or injection, major joint or bursa (e.g., shoulder, hip, knee or subacromial bursa with ultrasound guidance, with permanent recording and reporting). The code is billed with modifier -50, as it was a bilateral procedure. ICD-10 code M17.0 is for bilateral primary osteoarthritis of the knee.

18. **Answer: A**

CPT code 29824 represents Arthroscopy, shoulder, surgical; distal claviculectomy including distal articular surface (Mumford procedure).

Answer Key - 30,000 Series

19. **Answer: C**

    The mitral valve is the valve between the left atrium and the left ventricle of the heart, which has two tapered cusps.

20. **Answer: A**

    Needle puncture of Pleura to perform the drainage should be coded with CPT 32400.

21. **Answer: C**

    CPT 32551 represents "Tube thoracostomy, includes connection to the drainage system, when performed, open".

22. **Answer: C**

    As the surgeon removed the tissue from anterior ethmoid sinus, CPT code 31254 should be used. CPT code 31255 can be used, if the surgeon removed the tissue from both anterior and posterior ethmoid sinus, which is not the case here.

23. **Answer: A**

    CPT 33511 represents CABG with 2 venous grafts. Also, to code for endoscopic saphenous vein graft, use CPT 33508.

24. **Answer: D**

    As the ICU physician has performed Bronchoscopy + BAL and TBNA, the correct codes would be CPT 31624 and 31629.

25. **Answer: B**

    CPT code 30115 is the correct code because use of snare technique to remove the nasal polyps make it an extensive procedure.

26. **Answer: C**

    CPT code 31576 represents Laryngoscopy, flexible; with biopsy. This is correct code as a flexible laryngoscope was used for the procedure.

27. **Answer: D**

    Tricuspid valve ring placement is considered as replacement. Correct CPT code 33465 as it represents "Replacement, tricuspid valve, with cardiopulmonary bypass".

Answer Key – 40,000 Series

28. **Answer: D**

    As the secondary adenoidectomy was performed on patient whose age is above 12 years, so, correct CPT is 42836

29. **Answer: C**

    As the appendectomy was done as an open procedure and it was for ruptured appendix, use CPT 44960.

30. **Answer: B**

    CPT code 45380 represents "Colonoscopy, flexible; with biopsy, single or multiple". This includes the single or multiple biopsies throughout the colon, so no additional code is required.

31. **Answer: C**

    CPT code 47538 is the correct code as it includes the CPT 47532 (Injection procedure for cholangiography, percutaneous, complete diagnostic procedure including imaging guidance (eg, ultrasound and/or fluoroscopy) and all associated radiological supervision and interpretation; new access (eg, percutaneous transhepatic cholangiogram)) and it should not be billed separately.

32. **Answer: C**

    As the physician has performed Colonoscopy and dilated the strictures with a transendoscopic balloon, the correct code would be 45386.

33. **Answer: A**

    Freeing of intestinal adhesions is known as Enterolysis. As the surgeon did an open enterolysis, the correct code is CPT 44005.

34. **Answer: D**

    The spleen is an organ in the upper far left part of the abdomen, to the left of the stomach. The spleen is the largest organ in the lymphatic system and it acts as a filter for blood as part of the immune system.

35. **Answer: D**

    As the Snare technique was used to remove the polyps through colonoscopy, the correct CPT code is 45385.

36. **Answer: A**

CPT code 49652 is the correct code, as repair of umbilical hernia was done through Laparoscopy.

Answer Key - 50,000 Series

37. **Answer: B**

    Correct answer is B, as CPT code 59510 represents "Routine obstetric care including antepartum care, cesarean delivery, and postpartum care" and CPT code +59525 represents "Subtotal or total hysterectomy after cesarean delivery"

38. **Answer: D**

    As Provider performed treatment of ectopic pregnancy laparoscopically along with salpingectomy and oophorectomy, Correct CPT would be 59151.

39. **Answer: A**

    Correct CPT code is 57260 as Combined anteroposterior colporrhaphy was performed.

40. **Answer: C**

    The provider performed destruction of warts using cryosurgery, correct CPT code 54056 and correct code for radical orchiectomy through an inguinal incision is 54530.

41. **Answer: B**

    Fulguration was done for 0.3 cm lesion along with multiple biopsies, the correct CPT code would be 52224.

42. **Answer: B**

    Correct CPT codes are 50392, 74475.

43. **Answer: A**

    The prostate Biopsy was done using a needle under Fluoroscopic guidance, so the correct CPT codes are 55700, 77002.

44. **Answer: C**

    Correct code for Closure of vesicouterine fistula is CPT code 51920.

45. **Answer: A**

    Ureter is considered part of the Renal system but not of the Female Reproductive system.

46. **Answer: C**

    Correct answer is C, as Total abdominal hysterectomy was done along with removal of the tube(s) and ovary(s).

47. **Answer: B**

Correct answer is B, as the patient underwent TURP procedure and it is nowhere mentioned that it was a secondary operation (Regrowth or residual resection).

48. **Answer: A**

Correct answer is A, as no surgical procedure was done, and simply shock waves were given through the skin to break the kidney calculus in small fragments that can easily pass in urine.

Answer Key - 60,000 Series

49. Answer: C

Removal of lens material was done through pars plana approach. The correct code is CPT 66852.

50. Answer: A

CPT code 63042 represents Laminotomy (hemilaminectomy), with decompression of nerve root(s), including partial facetectomy, foraminotomy and/or excision of herniated intervertebral disc, reexploration, single interspace; lumbar

51. Answer: B

CPT code 63090 represents the Lumbar Vertebral corpectomy done through a transperitoneal approach. This code is applicable for 1 segment. For each additional segment, use add-on CPT code +63091.

52. Answer: A

Correct CPT code is 69636, Tympanoplasty with antrotomy or mastoidotomy; with ossicular chain reconstruction.

53. Answer: B

The surgeon performed left total thyroid lobectomy with isthmusectomy. The correct CPT code is 60220.

54. Answer: A

The correct code is 69200, Removal foreign body from external auditory canal; without general anesthesia.

55. Answer: C

Excision of Morton's neuroma should be coded with CPT code 28080.

56. Answer: D

The correct CPT code for injection of anesthetic agent in the phrenic nerve is 64410.

57. Answer: B

Adrenal glands is the correct answer, as they sit atop the kidneys.

58. Answer: A

Correct answer is A, as Iris expansion device was used, which makes it a complex surgery than routine cataract surgery.

59. Answer: C

Correct answer is C, as the Lumbar puncture was diagnostic in nature to rule out the disease.

60. Answer: B

Correct answer is B *"Laminectomy with exploration and/or decompression of spinal cord and/or cauda equina, without facetectomy, foraminotomy or discectomy (eg, spinal stenosis), 1 or 2 vertebral segments; lumbar, except for spondylolisthesis".*

Answer Key - Evaluation and Management

61. **Answer: B**

    A patient has made an Annual Wellness visit to his PCP. The correct code would be G0439 considering this as a routine AWV. Also PCP made a comprehensive History and examination, then he should code CPT 99215, as the code description states that only 2 of the three key components need to be met. Since the Comprehensive history and exam were met, this code can still be assigned.

62. **Answer: D**

    The correct codes for routine preventive checkup are CPT 99396 and ICD-10 CM code Z00.00.

63. **Answer: D**

    The correct way of reporting Critical Care services is to break down the Critical care time. For the first 30-74 min, use CPT code 99291 and for each additional 30 minutes, use 1 unit of CPT code +99292. In this case, the total time is 94 minutes. For the first 74 minutes, use 1 unit of CPT code 99291 and for the next (94-74) 20 minutes, use 1 unit of add-on codes +99291.

64. **Answer: A**

    The correct code is CPT 99284, because ER evaluation was done with comprehensive history; Detailed examination; and Medical decision making of moderate complexity.

65. **Answer: C**

    The correct CPT code is 99234.

66. **Answer: B**

    The correct CPT code is 99233, as the service is for an initial inpatient service that includes a comprehensive history and physical with a high level of medical decision making complexity.

67. **Answer: B**

    As routine checkup was done by Registered Nurse Practitioner, the correct code is 99211.

68. **Answer: C**

    Correct answer is C, as it was a consultation visit and all 3-Rs of Consultant visit (request, render and reply) were fulfilled.

69. Answer: C

Correct answer is C, as the age of the patient is 11 month, and CPT code 99471 should be reported for Critical Care provided to patients of 29 days through 24 months of age.

Answer Key - Anesthesia

70. Answer: C

Since the toddler's age is more than one year, the correct CPT is 00832.

71. Answer: B

Correct option is option B as CPT 01714 represents "Anesthesia for procedures on nerves, muscles, tendons, fascia, and bursae of upper arm and elbow; tenoplasty, elbow to shoulder" and P3 modifier is the correct P modifier for severe asthma. Also, as the patient age is above 70 yrs, so CPT code 99100 should be billed.

72. Answer: C

The P1 modifier describes an otherwise healthy individual and the question does not mention any anomaly or systemic condition in the patient.

73. Answer: B

As per the Anesthesia coding guidelines, "Time Reporting", anesthesia time begins when the anesthesiologist begins preparing the patient for the induction of anesthesia and ends when the anesthesiologist releases the patient from his care and is no longer in attendance. So Anesthesiologist should bill option B (1 hour 15 minutes = 75 minutes).

74. Answer: A

Correct answer is A, as Anesthesia was provided for CABG with a pump oxygenator.

75. Answer: D

Answer Key - Radiology

76. Answer: C

CPT Magnetic resonance (eg, proton) imaging, spinal canal and contents, without contrast material, followed by contrast material(s) and further sequences; lumbar, include both without and with contrast (followed).

77. Answer: B

Correct option is B, as procedure and injection were performed bilaterally.

78. Answer: B

As the Radiopharmaceutical localization using SPECT was done for the inflammatory process, the correct CPT is 78807.

79. Answer: A

80. Answer: B

81. Answer: B

As the radiofrequency ablation of one or more liver tumors were done percutaneously and under USG guidance, the correct CPT codes are 47382, 76940.

82. Answer: C

Correct answer is C, as CT scan was done without contrast material and lungs are a part of thorax.

83. Answer: A

Correct answer is A, as bilateral Mammography with CAD performed, was diagnostic in nature.

84. Answer: A

Correct answer is A, as total 7 seeds were placed directly inside the Prostate gland.

Answer Key - Laboratory / Pathology

85. Answer: C

As the Occult blood test was performed for other than colorectal neoplasm screening reasons, the correct CPT code is 82272.

86. Answer: A

The correct code for fecal Calprotectin is CPT 83993.

87. Answer: C

The CPT code 80053 represents Comprehensive metabolic panel This panel must include the following: Albumin (82040) Bilirubin, total (82247) Calcium, total (82310) Carbon dioxide (bicarbonate) (82374) Chloride (82435) Creatinine (82565) Glucose (82947) Phosphatase, alkaline (84075) Potassium (84132) Protein, total (84155) Sodium (84295) Transferase, alanine amino (ALT) (SGPT) (84460) Transferase, aspartate amino (AST) (SGOT) (84450) Urea nitrogen (BUN) (84520).

Calcium; ionized is not part of CMP, so it should be reported separately with CPT code 82330.

88. Answer: B

As comprehensive consultation with review of patients records and specimens was done, so the correct CPT code is 80502.

89. Answer: D

As all these labs tests are part of the Basic Metabolic panel, so there is no need to report these all separately. CPT code 80047 covers all these lab tests.

90. Answer: B

The CPT code 82951 includes 3 specimens (includes glucose) for Glucose tolerance test (GTT).

91. Answer: C

Correct answer is C, as the patient is already on blood thinner drugs, to rule out the coagulation factors, PT test was performed.

92. Answer: C

Correct answer is CPT code 80047, 82140 as Basic Metabolic Panel and Ammonia tests were performed.

93. **Answer: C**

Correct answer is C as the autopsy was done for forensic purpose, i.e., for legal or medical reasons.

Answer Key - Medicine

94. **Answer: C**

    The correct answer is CPT code 97033 (Application of a modality to 1 or more areas; iontophoresis, each 15 minutes).

95. **Answer: A**

    The correct code for Rabies Immune globulin, Human, IM/SC is 90375.

96. **Answer: B**

    The correct answer is option B, as the IV Hydration was given for 50 minutes.

97. **Answer: A**

    The correct Codes are CPT 92924 and 92923, as the PTCA Angioplasty was done in Left main Coronary artery, whereas the Intracoronary stents were placed in the left circumflex artery.

98. **Answer: B**

    The correct codes for Hydration (for Dehydration treatment) are CPT 96360, 96361.

99. **Answer: D**

    As the psychotherapy was provided for 30 minutes, the correct code is CPT 90832.

100. **Answer: A**

     Correct answer is A.

101. **Answer: B**

     Correct answer is B, as Allergist prepared and injected 3 single-dose allergens in the patient.

102. **Answer: B**

     Correct answer is B, as Gastroenterologist has performed Capsule endoscopy of whole GI Tract.

Answer Key - Medical Terminology

103. Answer: B

Chondroblastoma of the proximal humerus is still sometimes referred to as Codman's Tumor.

104. Answer: A

Pulmonary veins are the only veins which carry oxygenated blood from lungs to the left atrium of the heart.

105. Answer: B

106. Answer: C

A rheumatologist is an internist or pediatrician who received further training in the diagnosis (detection) and treatment of musculoskeletal disease and systemic autoimmune conditions commonly referred to as rheumatic diseases.

107. Answer: C

Myringotomy is surgical incision into the eardrum, to relieve pressure or drain fluid.

108. Answer: B

The electroretinography (ERG) is a diagnostic test that measures the electrical activity generated by neural and non-neuronal cells in the retina in response to a light stimulus.

109. Answer: C

Onychomycosis is clinical terms used for fungal infection of the nails.

110. Answer: B

A thoracostomy is a small incision of the chest wall, with maintenance of the opening for drainage.

111. Answer: C

Arthon is a greek word for Joint.

Answer Key - Anatomy

112. Answer: A

The choroid coat, also known as the choroid or choroidea, is the vascular layer of the eye, containing connective tissues, and lying between the retina and the sclera.

113. Answer: D

Osteosarcoma is a type of cancer that produces immature bone. It is the most common type of cancer that arises in bones, and it is usually found at the end of long bones, often around the knee.

114. Answer: C

The hamate is a wedge-shaped carpal bone. It is located on the outside area of the wrist, which is the same side as the pinkie finger.

115. Answer: C

Ileum is the third portion of the small intestine, between the jejunum and the caecum.

116. Answer: B

Xenograft is a tissue graft or organ transplant from a donor of a different species from the recipient.

117. Answer: B

Obturator Nerve innervates the muscles of the medial compartment of the thigh (obturator externus, adductor longus, adductor brevis, adductor magnus and gracilis).

118. Answer: A

Human Heart has 4 valves. Mitral valve, Tricuspid valve, Aortic valve and Pulmonary valve.

119. Answer: A

The cecum or caecum is a pouch within the peritoneum that is considered to be the beginning of the large intestine.

120. Answer: C

Prostate is a walnut-sized gland located between the bladder and the penis.

Answer Key - ICD-10 CM Diagnosis

121. **Answer: A**

    Correct answer is Z71.6 for Tobacco abuse counseling.

122. **Answer: C**

    The correct codes are U07.1, R05, R06.0.

123. **Answer: A**

    The correct ICD-10 CM code for spiral fracture of the shaft of left humerus is S42.325A.

124. **Answer: B**

    Correct ICD-10 CM codes are R07.9, V74.5XXA

125. **Answer: B**

126. **Answer: C**

    The correct codes are ICD-10 CM L02.234 and B95.8.

127. **Answer: A**

    The correct codes are M84.661A, Q78.0.

128. **Answer: B**

    As the Viral meningitis is due to HIV infection, use ICD-10 CM codes B20 and A87.8.

129. **Answer: A**

    Correct Answer is Z20.828, as the friend of the patient, whom he came in contact with, has a confirmed case of COVID-19.

130. **Answer: A**

    Correct answer is A, as the reason for the encounter was management of an anemia associated with the malignancy.

131. **Answer: A**

    Correct answer is E11.9 as the patient is with Diabetes Mellitus without any complication.

132. **Answer: B**

    Correct answer is B, as the Carbuncle is on the left lower limb.

Answer Key - HCPCS Level II

133. Answer: A

E1: A service was performed on the upper left eyelid

134. Answer: D

Correct HCPCS code Fluorouracil is J9190.

135. Answer: A

The correct HCPCS code range is A5500-A5513.

136. Answer: E1195

The correct HCPCS code is E1195

137. Answer: D

HCPCS P series codes include Pathology and Laboratory services.

138. Answer: C

Right Thumb is identified by using the F5 HCPCS level II Modifier.

Answer Key - Coding Guidelines

139. Answer: True

140. Answer: True

141. Answer: C

CPT codes are copyrighted by AMA.

142. Answer: C

CM stands for Clinical Modification in ICD-10 CM codes.

143. Answer: A

As per the medicare coding guidelines, the correct answer is New Patient E/M Codes (99201 - 99205).

144. Answer: A

As per ICD-10 CM guideline Exclue 1 codes cannot be billed together.

Answer Key - Compliance and Regulatory

145. Answer: C

Medical necessity is what adjudicates, or justifies, a claim for payment.

146. Answer: D

Medicare Part B is outpatient insurance and helps cover office visits and consultation services.

147. Answer: B

The HCFA 1500 form is the standard claim form used by a non-institutional provider or supplier to bill Medicare carriers and durable medical equipment regional carriers (DMERCs) when a provider qualifies for a waiver from the Administrative Simplification Compliance Act (ASCA) requirement for electronic submission of claims.

148. Answer: B

POS 22 represents "On Campus Outpatient Hospital" - A portion of a hospital's main campus which provides diagnostic, therapeutic (both surgical and nonsurgical), and rehabilitation services to sick or injured persons who do not require hospitalization or institutionalization.

149. Answer: B

HIPAA stands for Health Insurance Portability and Accountability Act of 1996.

150. Answer: D

Employment status does not qualify for PHI under HIPAA rules.

PRACTICE TEST #2

10,000 Series

1. A 17-year-old male with cutaneous abscess of right axilla scheduled today for incision and drainage of the abscess. Estimated blood loss 5 ml. Incision and drainage of the right axilla abscess completed. Swab culture was taken. Cavity washed with H_2O_2 and iodoform is inserted.
    a. 10060
    b. 10061
    c. 10040
    d. 10080

2. **Preoperative Diagnosis:** Bedsores
    Postoperative Diagnosis: Bedsores
    Procedure: Debridement of sacral decubitus

    Indication of the surgery:
    A 64-year-old male follow up for Grade 4 bedsores. Patient underwent debridement, under general anesthesia, and daily dressing with soaked betadine gauze.

    Procedure Details:
    Patient consented to the procedure. Complications discussed, understood. Agreed to surgery. All questions answered to satisfaction.

    Patient in a left lateral decubitus position. Sacral area prepped and draped. Washout of the area and debridement performed. Sterile dressing. The patient tolerated the procedure well, transferred to the recovery room in good condition.
    a. 11046
    b. 11044
    c. 11043
    d. 11047

3. A 39-year-old male with a tender soft mobile mass on the right side of the trunk area for years. Recently painful, tender, and interrupting sleep for two days. Excision of the lesion from the right side of the trunk measuring 8.9 cm. CPT code is:

a. 11406
   b. 11404
   c. 11403
   d. 11401

4. A 46-year-old male with a sebaceous cyst on the abdomen scheduled for fine-needle aspiration biopsy. Inserted 18-gauge needle with attached syringe into the suspicious lesion, collected tissue. Sent to pathology to check the malignancy. CPT code is:
   a. 10004
   b. 10021
   c. 10005
   d. 10006

5. A patient with oblique skin cut on the radial aspect of basic phalanx of left index finger without affecting any tendons and bones. Scheduled for simple repair of wound. In supine position, cleaning of left hand and index finger. Inspection of wound. No defect in tendons or bones. It is only a superficial oblique longitudinal skin cut less than two cm. Skin closure completed, one with Ethilon 3-0. Jelonet dressing and butterfly plaster applied. Skin suture removal after 10-12 days. CPT code is:
   a. 12002-F1
   b. 12004-F1
   c. 12005-F1
   d. 12001-F1

6. A 33-year-old female with malignant neoplasm of nipple and areola scheduled for removal of breast lesion. General anesthesia administered. Sentinal lymph node dissection completed. Segmental resection and oncoplastic reconstruction of right breast. Frozen came back as benign lymph node and margins are clear; 19 JP drain is left behind. Skin closure performed.
   a. 19112-RT
   b. 19110-RT
   c. 19120-RT
   d. 19125-RT

7. A 45-year-old female presented with two painful, itchy, bleeding masses on neck and left submammary area for two months. The lesion is increasing in size with tenderness and

discomfort, surrounding irritation, bleeding, and redness. The biggest lesion on the submammary measures 2 cm in size and 0.5 cm lesion on the neck. Physician excised two lesions under complete aseptic technique. Applied local infiltration anesthesia 1 ml lidocaine with epinephrine, subcutaneous below the lesions. Simple repair completed to close the wounds. Correct CPT code is:
   a. 11403, 11420, 12001
   b. 11402, 11420-59
   c. 11404, 11420
   d. 11404, 11420-59

8. A 55-year-old female with diabetic foot ulcer on the right foot for one year. Scheduled for debridement of the wound. The wound is less than 1 cm. There is no collection, drained by itself. Skin around is not inflamed and without secretion. Physician covered the wound with Aquacel Ag, debrided the wound. ICD-10 CM and CPT are:
   a. 11042, E11.621, L97.519
   b. 11045-RT, E11.621, L97.519
   c. 11042-RT, E11.621, L97.519
   d. 11042-RT, E11.9, L97.519

9. A 32-year-old male scheduled for scar conditions and fibrosis of skin. Insertion of tissue expanders and grafting performed. General anesthesia administered. Placed in supine position. Given pre-operated Cefazolin. Prepped and draped. Harvesting of fat 110 cc from abdomen.

   Pocket made for expander; hemostasis achieved. 70x95x50 mm and volume 270 ml inserted, injected 27 ml-size 12 drains inserted. Closed with Vicryl 4/0 and Monocryl 4/0. Fibrosis debrided from the old scar, Nano fat 40 ml, and microfat-100ml injected in two layers. Wound closed with Jalonet, plain gauze, and crepe bandage applied. CPT codes are:
   a. 11960, 15770-59, L90.5
   b. 11960, 15770-59, 11042-59, L90.5
   c. 19357, 15570-59, L90.5
   d. 11960, 15570-59, L90.5

20,000 Series

10. A 30-year-old male scheduled for fracture of nasal bones, initial encounter. Closed treatment of nasal septal fracture performed. Fracture reduced by digital pressure with satisfactory results. Thermal splint applied. No skin closure. No blood.
    a. 21336, S02.2XXD
    b. 21337, S02.2XXA
    c. 21336, S02.2XXA
    d. 21337, S02.2XXD

11. A 27-year-old male with a displaced scaphoid fracture. Left wrist scheduled for procedure. Placed in supine position under general anesthesia. Draped and controlled under C-arm for the positioning of reduction in hyperextension. Checking the entry point and opening the skin 5 mm at the palmar side of scaphoid bone right over the tuberosities. Placed guide pin on the tip of the bone and controlling all directions. Drilling through the distal fragment and reducing by bending and radial adduction of the hand. Placing central, the guide pin in the proximal fragment. Measuring a 20-mm headless screw, and control of the fracture reduction under C-arm. Perfect grip and closing of the fracture gap. Removal of the guide pin, final C-arm control, and documentation. Washing procedure and closing the wound with 5-Ethilon. Dry dressing and reapplication of the short-arm splint with thumb. Early wound control and x-ray control recommended in one week.
    a. 25685-RT
    b. 25676-RT
    c. 25680-RT
    d. 25690-RT

12. Patient complains of right foot pain. Pain increased in severity with activities. Patient tried conservative treatment in the form of rest, medications, and injections without any relief. Examination revealed tenderness of the medial aspect of the right foot at the outer surface of the navicular bone with swelling. X-ray evidenced accessory of navicular bone. Procedure completed for reconstruction posterior tibial tendon, excision of accessory of navicular bone. What is the CPT code for the procedure performed?
    a. 28230-RT
    b. 28232-RT
    c. 28238-RT
    d. 28234-RT

13. Patient is scheduled for removal of deep implant. Spinal anesthesia administered. Sterilization, 2 cm incision on previous scar on left upper tibia. Removed screw from tibial tunnel. Closed and dressed wound. No postoperative complications. CPT code is:
    a. 20680-LT
    b. 20670-LT
    c. 20665-LT
    d. 20664-LT

14. Patient has a localized neck lesion of 3 cm scheduled for excision of the lesion. Incision on the mass, right side of the neck. After dissection, the lesion marked on the right side of the neck. Lidocaine and adrenaline injected locally around the lesion. Incision completed on lump. Dissected and removed. Lump opened, contains white cheesy material inside. After hemostasis and dissection, wound closed with dermal sutures. Dressing and operation completed without complications. CPT code is:
    a. 21550
    b. 21555
    c. 21552
    d. 21556

15. Patient scheduled for amputation, thigh through femur. In supine position, fish-mouth like incision, dissection of the left femur, transverse ostectomy completed with electric saw ligation the superficial femoral vein; and artery dissection the sciatic nerve, and squeezing nerve end, insertion of 15 suction drainage, and suture of the fascia and subcutaneous tissue using Vicryl 2*0. Skin stapler and dressed. No postoperative complications.
    a. 27580
    b. 27592
    c. 27590
    d. 27594

16. **Pre-Operative diagnosis:** Non-union fracture, right clavicle
    Post-Operative diagnosis: Non-union fracture, right clavicle

    Planned Procedure: Osteotomy clavicle with or without internal fixation
    Procedure Performed: Osteotomy clavicle with or without internal fixation W/B1 GRF NON/MAL

    Procedure Details:
    After induction, patient placed on a simple radiolucent table with slightly raised head and shoulders. After painting and draping, direct anterior exposure of the right clavicle. Hemostasis achieved. Previous implant was loose (plate/screws not holding). Implant removed along with the ss wire cerclage. Frank non-union confirmed with soft tissue

interposition. Fracture ends freshened after open reduction. Fixation achieved with an anatomical 7-hole lateral clavicle plate (AO-Synthes). A combination of cortical and locking screws used for fixation under fluoroscopic control. Bone grafting completed via freeze-dried cancellous bone chips packed into the fracture site. Closure done in layers. Estimated blood loss 50 ml.
- a. 23480-RT
- b. 23485-RT
- c. 23485-RT, 12031
- d. 23480-RT, 12031

17. A patient scheduled for follow up for non-displaced fracture of distal phalanx of left little finger. Internal fixation previously completed few weeks prior. Patient scheduled for the removal of deep implantation. AE cast removed. Incision performed, deep dissection down to visualized implant below the muscle level within bone. Both K wires removed after painting and draping. Wound cleaned, washed, and dressed. CPT and ICD codes are:
    - a. 20680-F4, S62.667D
    - b. 20680-F1, S62.667A
    - c. 20670-F4, S62.667A
    - d. 20670-F4, S62.667D

18. **Operation Performed:** Arthroscopic chondroplasty, repair meniscus major, bone graft iliac crest left knee.

    Procedure Details:
    Arthroscope through lateral portal. Instrumentation through medial and suprapatellar portals. Patellar articular surface grade III chondromalacia with fibrillation treated good effect with chondroplasty.

    Chondroplasty of the patella was completed followed by entrance into the medial compartment where there was a large ramp lesion of the medial meniscus repaired. Intercondylar notch, ACL intact including hook traction was performed. Lateral compartment focal area of hondromalacia anterolateral part of lateral tibial condyle treated with chondroplasty. Stem cells harvested from the right iliac crest were injected under direct vision into the area of patellar chondromalacia + 15 mL of 0.5% Marcaine. Nylon to all three portals. Vellban crepe bandage. Patient under observation, barring no complications, patient will be released tomorrow. CPT codes are:
    - a. 29870-LT, 20902-LT
    - b. 29882-LT, 20900-59-LT
    - c. 29882-LT, 20902-59-LT
    - d. 29880-LT, 20902-59-LT

30,000 Series

19. Patient with nodules of vocal cords scheduled for Microlaryngoscopy with excision of vocal cord lesions. Under general anesthesia ET intubation performed. Laryngoscope inserted. Microscope applied and right anterior vocal cord polyp seen. Epinephrine applied and polyp excised, sent for histopathology. Patient observed every two hours. CPT code is:
    a. 31536
    b. 31540
    c. 31545
    d. 31541

20. Patient with varicose veins of left lower extremities with pain underwent Endovenous Laser Ablation Therapy with phlebectomy left leg under local anesthesia. In supine position. Leg prepped and draped. Angio-access was gained at mid-thigh under ultrasound guidance. Laser fiber introduced through 4Fr sheath and advanced towards the groin. Tip of fiber placed approximately 2 cm study from saphenofemoral junction. Peri-venous tumescent anesthesia administered. Dilated incompetent GSV, laser ablated throughout from mid-thigh towards the junction with LEED. Post-procedural ultrasound showed a widely patent and compressible femoral vein. Previously marked varicose veins were excised through stab avulsions incisions. Wounds closure with Prolene 5-0 suture. Legs compressions with elastic stockings. No postoperative complications.
    a. 36478-LT, 37765-LT, 59
    b. 36478-LT, 36478-LT, 59
    c. 37765-LT
    d. 36478-LT

21. **Preoperative Diagnosis:** Left breast cancer

    Postoperative Diagnosis: Left breast cancer

    Procedure: 1. Ultrasound-guided venous access port placement.

    2. Fluoroscopy.

    Anesthesia: General anesthesia with endotracheal intubation

    Disposition: To the Recovery Room and then to the Floor

    Indication of the Surgery: A 41-year-old female, with cancer in the left breast. The patient scheduled for Port-A-Cath placement.

    Intraoperative Findings: The intraoperative findings showed nothing significant.

Procedure:
The patient was given antibiotic. The patient was prepped and draped. Ultrasound-guided access of the left internal jugular vein has been identified. The needle was introduced. The guidewire was not introduced to the superior vena cava. Completed through the right subclavian vein. The guidewire introduced. Dilators and catheter were introduced 15 cm from the skin area, tunneled subcutaneously in the pocket in the right subclavian area. Port secured in place, and fluoroscopy confirmed in good position. Good inflow and outflow noted. Good hemostasis. No complications. Closure using 3-0 Vicryl and 4-0 Monocryl for the skin. Patient tolerated the procedure. The patient transferred to the recovery room in good condition. Chest x-ray requested. Chemotherapy can begin after the x-ray is complete. The patient discharged if no complications.
   a. 36561, 76937, 31500
   b. 36561, 77001, 31500
   c. 36561, 77001, 76937
   d. 36561, 77001, 77001

22. **Pre-Operative Diagnosis:** End-stage renal disease
    Post-Operative Diagnosis: End-stage renal disease
    Procedure: Anteriovenous anastomosis, open

    Procedure details:
    Under tourniquet, lazy S incision. Cephalic vein dissected to previous anastomosis in mid-forearm. Vein divided distally. Radial artery exposed in cubital fossa; artery torutuous. After applying clamps, ulnar pulses remained confirming it is radial. Adventitia was cleared, vena commitans cut between ligatures. Arteriotomy completed, bit/edge was excised for better patency. Vein was opened 1 cm. Arteiotomy 9 mm. Hepain flush, correct orientation to avoid twisting. Anastomosis completed via parachuting technique for the heel area and continued to the toes. Good patency, flow on deflation of tourniquet. Surgical pieces kept protecting the anastomotic line. Final hemostasis completed. Vein placed in lazy curve without kinks. Elbow flexed to confirm that flow remains good. Final closure in two layers.
       a. 36821
       b. 36823
       c. 36820
       d. 36825

23. A patient with varicose veins of left lower leg scheduled for sclerotic injection. Patient prepped. Insertion of a syringe filled with a sclerosing solution directly into the affected veins (more than one incompetent vein of the same leg). Multiple injections were performed using foam 0.75+ 1.0% Aethoxysklerol. Removed needle. Applied pressure.
    a. 36465-LT
    b. 36471-LT
    c. 36470-LT
    d. 36468-LT

24. **Preoperative Diagnosis:** Respiratory failure secondary to infection and sepsis

    Postoperative Diagnosis: Respiratory failure secondary to infection and sepsis

    Procedure: Tracheostomy

    Procedure details:

    The patient consented to the procedure through family. Possible complications explained. Understood and agreed to proceed with surgery. Questions answered to satisfaction. The patient intubated. Sterilization and draping of the neck. Trachea localized. Transverse incision completed down to the subcutaneous tissue. The muscles and thyroid opened craniocaudally. Trachea hook placed. Stay-sutures applied. Trachea opened. A size 7.5 tracheostomy tube cuff placed with inflation of the balloon, secured in place. Skin stitched using 0 Protene. Pack left behind. No complications. The patient tolerated the procedure and sent to recovery room in good condition.

    a. 31600
    b. 31601
    c. 31603
    d. 31605

25. Patient scheduled for radiofrequency ablation and phlebectomy for his right leg symptomatic varicose veins. Placed in supine position, infiltration of 5 ml 2% lignocaine applied around the knee. Ultrasound-guided puncture of long saphenous vein completed. Insertion of 7-French introducer completed. Infiltration of cold saline + 30 ml 2% lignocaine + NaHo3 completed.

    Application of RF 1.5 cm distal to sephenofemoral junction completed. Post RF ablation DUPLEX showed no DVT. Phlebectomy completed with 18 stab incisions. Steri-strips applied. Elastic stocking applied. Correct CPT codes are:
    a. 36476-RT, 37765-59-RT
    b. 36476-RT, 37766-59-RT
    c. 36475-RT, 37766-59-RT
    d. 36475-RT, 37765-59-RT

26. **Planned Procedure:**   Repair of nasal septum
    Procedure Performed: Repair of nasal septum

    Procedure Details:
    Patient placed in supine position under general anesthesia. Face prepared and draped. Infiltration of nasal septum and inferior turbinates completed with 2% xylocaine and lidocaine. Incision 1 cm of posterior caudal septum margin. Elevation mucoperichondrealand mucoperosteal flap completed. Topical vasoconstrictive agents applied. Incision of cartilage. Removed deviation cartilaginous and osseous part of the nasal septum. Preserved a L-strut of 1.2 cm dorsal and causal septal. Trans-septal sutures. Mucoperichondrial sutures. Lateralization of left inferior turbinate. Same procedure completed on other side of inferior turbinate. Uncinate process removed. CPT codes are:
    a. 30520, 30140*2
    b. 30520, 30140
    c. 30520, 30140*2
    d. 30520, 30140

27. A 25-year-old female complaining of left-sided neck lumps, tender, slowly growing, and itchiness. Ultrasound of neck shown multiple enlarged confluent and discrete round to oval-shaped lymph nodes showing heterogeneous echo pattern and partial loss of fatty hilum seen involving left side of neck. Excisional biopsy of cervical lymph nodes completed under local anesthesia and sedation. Linear vertical incision completed with 2 cm. Lymph nodes excised and specimen sent for biopsy. The incision is repaired with a layered closure.
    a. 38500
    b. 38505
    c. 38510
    d. 38520

40,000 Series

28. The patient presented with chronic anal fissure refractory to medical therapy. She indicates constipation and rectal bleeding. Treatment options discussed. Patient elected to proceed with surgical intervention. The procedure indication, benefits, alternative, risks, and complications were reviewed. Patient understood and elected to proceed with surgery.

    The patient was brought to the operating room, given spinal anesthesia. Patient placed in the prone Jackknife position. All extremities were padded. The anal and perianal areas were then exposed by retracting the buttocks laterally and securing them in place with tape. Sterile prep and drape. Final surgical timeout completed.

    Visual inspection revealed multiple hemorrhoids and chronic posterior anal fissure with a tag. Rectum irrigated with saline. Rigid proctoscopy performed up to 15 cm. The fissure was excised posterior and central portion was debrided. Wound irrigated with betadine. A 1 cm transverse incision made over the intersphincteric groove in the left lateral aspect and the internal sphincter muscle was identified from the submucosal and the intersphinteric side. Approximately 6 mm of the fibers of the internal sphincter muscle released enough to cover the length of the fissure, 0.5% Marcaine was used for a wound block. Gelfoam soaked in Fucidin ointment was placed inside the anal canal followed by dry dressing.
    a. 46200, 45300-59
    b. 46083, 45300-59
    c. 46221, 45300-59
    d. 46200, 45303-59

29. A patient who is suffering from fourth-degree hemorrhoids underwent hemorrhoidopexy by stapling. What is the CPT code?
    a. 46946
    b. 46947
    c. 46948
    d. 46945

30. **Procedure:** Transanal full-thickness excision of anorectal polyp
    Anesthesia: General endotracheal
    Estimated Blood loss: 10 ml

    Indication of Surgery:
    The patient presented with incidental flat polyp at the anorectal junction. Various treatment options were discussed with him and he elected to proceed with surgical excision.

Description of Procedure:
The patient was brought to the operating room, given general endotracheal anesthesia. Placed in the prone Jackknife position. All extremities were padded. The anal and perianal areas were then exposed by retracting the buttocks laterally and securing them in place with tape. Sterile prepping and draping performed. Final surgical time out completed, 0.5% Marcaine. Anorectum irrigated with betadine. Small non-inflamed internal hemorrhoids. Patient had a flat lesion at the anterolateral aspect of the anal canal at dentate line and going superiorly. It was soft, non-ulcerated, and nontender, 1-1.5 cm in size. The area was raised with 1% lidocaine 1:100000 epinephrine. Excision was delineated with 2 to 3 mm gross margin all around. It was excised in full thickness to the level.
   a. 45172
   b. 45171
   c. 45160
   d. 45190

31. A 35-year-old male with chronic tonsillitis scheduled for tonsillectomy. Incision made at tonsillar pillars. General anesthesia administered. Mouth opened by gag and fixed with rods. Throat pack inserted. Left tonsil dissected by ENT forceps and removed. Later right tonsil dissected via same procedure. Hemostasis achieved. Mouth washed with saline. Throat pack removed. No complications. Soft diet dietary instructions.
    a. 42825, J35.01
    b. 42825, J35.02
    c. 42826, J35.02
    d. 42826, J35.01

32. **Preoperative Diagnoses:** Incisional ventral hernia
    Postoperative Diagnoses: Incisional ventral hernia
    Procedures: Repair of incisional ventral hernia with mesh
    Anesthesia: General endotracheal with left-sided TAP block
    Estimated Blood loss: 100 ml

    Indication of surgery:
    The patient developed incisional ventral hernia which was symptomatic with pain. Various treatment options were discussed. Patient elected to proceed with surgical intervention.

    Description of procedure:
    The patient was brought to the operating room. General endotracheal anesthesia administered. Patient placed in the supine position. Urinary catheter inserted. A left-sided TAP block performed for postoperative pain control. Abdomen prepped and draped. Using a secondary oblique incision over the left lower quadrant, dissection through skin and subcutaneous tissue to the fascia. An incisional ventral hernia present. Loops of small bowel inside the hernia sac. Bowel reduced back inside the abdomen. Hernia sac excised. The

peritoneum closed with #0-Vicryl suture in a running fashion. The anterior fascia was of poor quality, mesh was necessary to reinforce the repair. The rectus sheath was lifted off the rectus muscle to create a subfascial plane posterior to the anterior sheath and the external oblique. Once the subfascial pocket was created and the piece of mesh was introduced in subfascial plane anterior to the rectus muscle. Trimmed to reduce size to fit area. Covered 7-8 cm area. Mesh secured to the anterior aspect of the muscle using a combination of 2-0 Prolene and 2-0 PDS. Prior to securing the mesh, the edge of the rectus muscle and internal oblique was approximated with 2-0 PDS in a running fashion. The anterior fascia was approximated over the mesh using a combination of 2-0 PDS in a running fashion and #1 PDS in a figure-of-eight fashion. Wound irrigated with Gentamycin impregnated solution. The subcutaneous fat was approximated with 2-0 Vicryl in a running fashion in two layers. The skin was approximated with subcuticular fashion after excising the excess skin. Dry dressing.
   a. 49561, 49570
   b. 49561, 49566
   c. 49561, 49568
   d. 49561, 49565

33. A patient with acute cholecystitis with chronic cholecystitis scheduled for laparoscopic cholecystectomy. 12 mm hasson trocar was placed in the umbilicus using an open technique. The abdomen was inflated to 15 mmHg CO_2 5 mm trocars x3 placed in the right subcostal area. Gallbladder was retracted. Omental adhesions and duodenum released from the gallbladder. Gallbladder severely infected and edema of the wall very severe. Cystic artery was clipped twice and then transected. Performed same for the cystic duct. Gallbladder dissected from liver bed. Flushed the site with saline solution. Placed in bag, then extracted. JP drain was placed. All trocars were removed. Fascia closed using 2/0 vicryl. The skin closed using 4/0 rapid.
   a. 47562
   b. 47563
   c. 47564
   d. 47570

34. Received a 29-year-old female patient with complaints of lower abdominal pain for seven hours. Diagnoses of acute appendicitis. Order and recommended surgery of laparoscopy appendectomy. General anesthesia administered. Patient placed in supine position. Cleaned and draped. Three laparoscopic incisions. Camera found acute inflamed appendix.

    Grasper and harmonic used. The mesoappendix transected. Two vicryl loops inserted at base of appendix. Appendix was transected and removed. Abdomen defalcated. Wound closed.
    a. 44970, K35.80
    b. 44950, K35.2
    c. 44960, K35.80
    d. 44955, K35.2

35. **Indication:** Recurrent attacks of abdominal pain in the right iliac fossa.
    Procedure: Colonoscopy

    Procedure details: Physical exam performed. Informed consent obtained. All risks (perforation, bleeding, infection, and adverse effects to the medication) explained. Benefits and alternatives explained. Patient connected to the monitoring devices, placed in the left lateral position. Continuous oxygen provided with nasal cannula. Patient sedated. Digital exam performed. Colonoscopy introduced into the rectum. Visualization of the terminal ileum. Scope removed. Examination of color, texture, anatomy, and integrity of the mucosa. Obtained tissue sample. Patient transferred to the recovery area. Patient in satisfactory condition.

    Findings: Colon normal at the point of insertion. No polyps, diverticulitis, no inflammation.
    a. 45385
    b. 45380
    c. 45382
    d. 45388

36. Patient suffers from fourth-degree hemorrhoids and anal polyp. Scheduled for hemorrhoidectomy and destruction of anal lesion. Estimated blood loss 3 ml. Presence of nodules in a classical position. Excision of two enlarged hemorrhoidal nodules under Vicryl 2.0 ties (Milligan M0rgan procedure). Excision/biopsy of an anal polyp at 6 O'clock. Hemostasis using soft spray mode. Dressed. No postoperative complications.
    a. 46260, 46922-59
    b. 46261, 46924-59
    c. 46262, 46917-59
    d. 46260, 46916-59

50,000 Series

37. A 31-year-old female with high-grade dysplasia of cervix received treatment for conization of cervix with dilation and curettage, loop electrode excision. Transvaginal incision completed. Vulva and vagina cleaned and draped. Descending branches of the uterine artery ligated. Lugol iodine applied. Lugol negative areas around the cervical crater. Large loop was chosen, and cone cutout included all lugol iodine negative areas. Minimal bleeding. Cauterization of the cone crater completed. Cone marked at 12, endocervical curetting performed. All material sent to histopathology. Cone crater checked for hemostasis. No bleeding. No postoperative complications. Normal dietary instructions.
    a. 57520
    b. 57522
    c. 57513
    d. 57511

38. **Preoperative Diagnosis:** Bilateral undescended testicle
    Postoperative Diagnosis: Bilateral undescended testicle

    Procedure Performed: Orchiopexy inguinal approach with or without hernia repair

    Procedure Details:
    General anesthesia administered. Right side rockey davis incision. Camper and scarpa dissected. Dissection of the spermatic cord completed. Dissection of right testicle completed. Orchiopexy completed on right side by creating pouch for testicle. Incision of scrotum completed for left testicle and dissection of the left testicle completed. Fixation of the left testicle performed. Proper hemostasis. Layers are closed. Skin closure performed. Right inguinal incision, scarpus layer divided. External oblique divided testicle in mid-inguinrowal region. Tunica vaginalis incised. Vas and cord freed, tunneled into subdartuos pouch anchored with 4/0 PDS on both sides. Scrotal skin closed with 4/0 monocryl. External oblique, scarpus closed 4/0 vicryl. Left side scrotal incision tunica vaginalis opened; 3/0 PDS anchoring stitches the sides. Skin closed with 4/0 PDS; 5 CC Marcain skin infiltration completed.

    Postoperative instructions: Routine observation every hour. Provide clear diet after four hours. Proceed if tolerated.
    a. 54650-RT, 54650-LT
    b. 54640
    c. 54640-RT, 54640-LT
    d. 54650

39. A 52-year-old male with elevated prostate-specific antigen (PSA) and enlarged prostate, provider performed prostate biopsy. Samples removed from the prostate gland with a biopsy needle to be tested for cancer or other abnormal cell growth. Tissue samples sent to pathology for further examination.
    a. 55720
    b. 55706
    c. 55705
    d. 55700

40. A female patient with chronic salpingitis scheduled for laparoscopic excision of ovarian cystic lesions. In lithotomy position, Foley catheter and uterine mobilize applied. Direct entry through the umbilicus with clear vision over the abdomen. Upper abdomen and appendix healthy. Uterus normal in size and shape. Pouch of Douglas free. Left cystic lesion-hydatida cyst-attached to the ampullar part of the fallopian tube. Excised in line with the healthy tube, then filament adhesions released between the tube and the IP ligament. Right endometriotic node in the space between the isthmic part of the fallopian tube and the round ligament. Excised in full, no bleeding or damage to the tube. Specimens collected for histopathology. Methylene blue injected shows free passage of the right tube and passage of the dye until the ampula of the left tube. Anti-joint gel applied as antiadhesive. Airseal extraction.
    a. 58661
    b. 58662
    c. 58660
    d. 58670

41. **Indication:** Left tubal ectopic pregnancy

    Procedure Details:
    General anesthesia administered. In lithotomy position urine catheter inserted. Laparoscopy with 2 trocars 10 mm and 5 mm inserted without complications. In the pelvic there is a bulky looking uterus extremely retroverted. Mild amount of blood in the Douglas. The left side, on the adnexa, there is a tubal left ectopic pregnancy. Left ovary is normal. Left tube is opened. Ectopic pregnancy removed and extracted in an endobag and sent to pathology. Hemostasis controlled on the tube. No complications. No bleeding. On the right adnexa, right tube and ovary are normal. Douglas is free of lesions. Peritoneal wash with normal saline. No complications during or after surgery.
    a. 59150
    b. 59151
    c. 59140
    d. 59136

42. A male patient with other hydronephrosis and laparoscopic pyeloplasty, and cystourethroscopy, with insertion of indwelling ureteral stent procedure scheduled. General anesthesia administered. Prepped and draped. 18 French Foley catheter inserted. Patient positioned in a right flank position 60° and fixed to the operative table, care given to all pressure points. 11 mm camera port was inserted from the umbilicus in open technique. Pneumo-peritoneum completed, and insertion of another 5 mm and 10 mm trochars were completed under direct vision in a V-shaped manner with a camera port. Reflection of the right descending colon performed medially with sharp and blunt dissection using harmonic scalpel. Care taken with the bowel until IVC visualized. The section performed caudally on the IVC identifying the ureter. Resection was carried out caudally until the site of impending of the ureter behind IVC. Further dissection started on the renal pelvis down to the point where it lies behind IVC laterally. Freeing of the ureter from behind IVC completed. The ureter brought anterior to the IVC and spatulation was performed on both ends of the proximal and distal of the ureter. 6 French 24 cm JJ was inserted. Ureter was re-anastomosed with anterior and posterior layers of running 4-0 Vicryl tightly fashioned. On completing the procedure hemostasis was insured and a JJ stent was in position. All the ports withdrawn under direct vision showing no bleeding and pneumo-peritoneum was deflated. Aerocoele machine was used to minimize any spillage. No operative complication. Patient tolerated the procedure well. Transferred to PACU stable. Estimated blood loss of 50 ml.
    a. 50543, 52332
    b. 50545, 52332
    c. 50544, 52332
    d. 50544, 52330

43. A 30-years-old female scheduled for surgical treatment of missed abortion in first trimester with gestational age of seven weeks of her pregnancy. What is the CPT code?
    a. 59821
    b. 59820
    c. 59830
    d. 59840

44. **Preoperative diagnosis:** Rectocele
    Postoperative diagnosis: Rectocele
    Procedure: Rectocele repair and vaginal defect repair

    Procedure details:
    Hydro dissection of the rectovaginal space performed. Dissection of the posterior vaginal mucosa till mid-vagina performed. Tightening of muscles on both sides in four levels to one cm above the interoitus by interrupted simple vicryl 2/0. Excision of mucosal excess performed. V-shape incision on the perineum to one cm above the anal margin. Peeling of the skin performed. Suturing and reproaching of both sides by vicryl 2/0. Closure of the

vaginal mucosa with vicryl 2/0 continuously to the fourchetee. Closure of the skin of the perineum in two layers by vicryl rapid 3/0. PR performed and is normal. Urine clear. No bleeding. Vaginal pack inserted. Vaginal pack will be removed by tomorrow.
   a. 57250, 57285
   b. 57250, 57284
   c. 57240, 57285
   d. 57240, 57284

45. A 25-year-old male patient with lower abdominal pain and full bladder. Has frequency and urgency more during daytime. Nocturia 1-2 times. Seen, examined, and uroflow. Emptied bladder with complex procedure by electronic equipment and recorded the volume of urine per minute. Test results were discussed and advised to try cutting fluids. Final diagnosis: overactive bladder. Correct CPT code is:
    a. 51736, N32.81
    b. 51726, N32.81
    c. 51725, N32.81
    d. 51741, N32.81

46. A female patient's left Bartholin cyst is growing in size. The cyst painful and uncomfortable. Scheduled for removal of Bartholin cyst. Vertical incision of the left labia majora, facing the Bartholin cyst. Dissection of the Bartholin cyst in toto. Excision of the Bartholin cyst performed. Profuse washing with diluted betadine. Content of the cyst sent to culture. Results of culture; mildly pustulent. Closure via plane by plane with vicryl 2/0. Skin closure via vicryl 3/0. No postoperative complications. Dietary instruction given.
    a. 56740, 12001
    b. 56740, 12001-59
    c. 56740
    d. 56740, 12011-59

47. A 27-year-old female 33 weeks pregnant with the pregnancy complication of antepartum hemorrhage. Growth scan performed. Gestational age is 33 weeks and 6 days. Informed labor room for cesarean delivery only. Estimated blood loss 500 ml. Pfanenstiel incision performed. Abdomen opened in layers. Uterus incised, delivery of 33 weeks living baby boy performed. Placenta and membranes completely delivered by CCT. Uterus sutured in layers; hemostasis secured. Sheath sutured by continuous vicryl. Cubcuticularmonocryl to skin. No postoperative complications. Routine observation every 15 minutes for 4 hours.
    a. 59515
    b. 59525
    c. 59510
    d. 59514

48. **Planned Procedure**: Hysteroscopy Biopsy
    Procedure Performed: Hysteroscopy Biopsy
    Pre-Operative Diagnosis: Abnormal uterine and vaginal bleeding
    Post-Operative Diagnosis: Endometrial Hyperplasia

    Procedure Details:
    General anesthesia administered. Patient placed in lithotomy position. Dilation of cervix is up to hegar 6. Diagnostic hysteroscopy showing normal cavity uterus focal of thickened endometrium in some areas. Curettage performed; sample sent for histopathology specimen. No bleeding. No complications. Sent to recovery room in good condition.
    a. 58558
    b. 58562
    c. 58565
    d. 58560

60,000 Series

49. **Preoperative Diagnosis:** Right lobe suspicious nodule.
Postoperative Diagnosis: Right thyroid nodule
Procedure Performed: Right hemithyroidectomy
Anesthesia: General anesthesia with endotracheal intubation
Fluid Given: 1000 ml
Estimated blood loss: Minimal

Indication of the surgery:
A 35-yr-old female with history of PCOS currently taking Glucophage. Referred for a suspicious right inferior thyroid nodule, FNA reveals suspicious of follicular neoplasm category 4.

Intraoperative findings:
Intraoperative findings showed a right thyroid lobe nodule that was completely removed, sent for frozen section. Benign.

Procedure details:
Patient consented to the procedure. Patient understands potential complications. Patient agreed to surgery. Questions answered to satisfaction. Business card supplied.

The patient was positioned in a head-up position. The patient was intubated and prepped and draped. No muscle relaxant administered. Anti-DVT prophylaxis has been given.

Standard transverse incision above the sterna notch. Superior flap, inferior flap, and lateral flap created, down to pre-tracheal fascia. The right middle thyroid vein divided, and inferior pole divided using the ligature. Superior pole divided between clips and transfixing sutures. Recurrent laryngeal nerve identified and preserved. Good hemostasis. Good irrigation. Berry's ligament divided. The right thyroid lobe completely removed. Thyroid removed, sent for frozen section evaluation. Benign. Valsava maneuver performed 20/20, systolic reached >100. No oozing. The infesting of the deep cervical fascia was approximated with the strap muscles using 3-0 Vicryl as well as the subcutaneous tissue. The skin closed using 4-0 Monocryl. Dry sterile dressing. The patient tolerated the procedure well. No complications. Transferred to recovery room. Transferred to floor under observation for 24 hours. CPT code is:

a. 60220-RT
b. 60240-RT
c. 60220-RT, 31500
d. 60240-RT, 31500

50. **Preoperative Diagnosis:** Sciatica, left side
    Postoperative Diagnosis: Sciatica, left side

    Procedure Performed: Laminotomy with decompression of nerve roots
    Estimated Blood Loss: 10 ml

    Procedure Details:
    General anesthesia administered. Prone position, left paramedian incision performed over L5-S1. Left side interlaminar performed, partial drilling of the lamina of L5. Removed ligamentum flavum. S1 nerve root identified, pushed up toward and laterally by sequestrated disc. Herniation the disc accessed through the axilla of the nerve root, sequestrectomy was performed, nerve root was mobilized medically and microdiscectomy performed L5-S1. A calcified disc in this area, removed using Kerrison rongeurs at the end of the procedure. The nerve root completely freed. Clauser in anatomical layers without a drain after applying gentamicin Depo-Medrol and betamix. No postoperative complications.

    a. 63030, M54.32
    b. 63030, M54.31
    c. 63020, M54.32
    d. 63020, M54.31a

51. A patient with thyroid cyst scheduled to drain the cyst. Thyroid cyst examined. Patient positioned on back with the neck extended, pillow under patient's shoulder. Prepared the biopsy site, administered local anesthetic to numb the area. Cleaned the biopsy site and incises the skin. Inserted a needle through the incision and into the cyst, drained the cyst, collected a sample of fluid for testing. Applied a sterile dressing.

    a. 60500, E04.1
    b. 60281, E04.1
    c. 60300, E04.1
    d. 60502, E04.1

52. Patient with traumatic brain injury scheduled for cranioplasty skull defect more than 5 cm diameter. Patient in supine position, pillow under his left shoulder. Head tilted to the left side, incision over the old scar at the left frontal temporoparietal region. The edges of the bone flap identified. The temporalis muscle adherent over the dura. Dissection was quite difficult. A small CSF leak from the dura and bleeding from the middle meningeal artery branches. Temporalis muscle was preserved as much as possible and care was taken not to injure or work at the location of the fascial nerve. Sterile bone flap put back in position after putting layover dural substitute over the dural defects. Bone flap was fixed in position with stitches in 6 locations, hemostasis was performed. Closure in anatomical layers after placing the vacuum drain. No complications.
    a. 62141
    b. 62140
    c. 62142
    d. 62143

53. A 6-year-old patient with superficial foreign body of auditory canal scheduled for removal of the foreign body from right ear. Bluish bead in the right ear canal found. General anesthesia administered. Ear visualized by microscope, bead imbedded ear canal walls. Removed. Some bleeding from right ear canal walls. Bleeding stopped by adrenaline cotton balls, ciprobay antibiotic added. No complications.
    a. 69200-RT
    b. 69155-RT
    c. 69205-RT
    d. 69209-RT

54. A 54-year-old male with unspecified viral encephalitis scheduled for burr hole with biopsy of brain or intracranial lesion. General anesthesia administered. MRI of head, compatible meynfeild frame, neuronavigation used to calibrate the images. Entry point chosen to reach the target on the left frontal area, burr hole performed with pediatric drill head, the dura coagulated. Using navigation, the target accessed, and six specimens taken in different directions and lengths, 1 specimen sent for culture. Classical closure. No postoperative complications.
    a. 61140
    b. 61150
    c. 61151
    d. 61154

55. **Preoperative Diagnosis**: Keratoconus unstable.
    Postoperative Diagnosis: Keratoconus stable, Ferrara ring implant in cornea.
    Operation Performed: Keratoprosthesis
    Anesthesia Given: Local anesthesia.
    Complications: No complications
    Description of Operative Procedure:
    Patient in operative area, prepped and draped. Following this, a lid speculum placed between the two eyelids of the left eye. Marking of the visual axis performed with Sinskey Hook. Tunnel zone demarcated 5.0 mm from the visual axis. Stromal incision performed via diamond knife. Tunnel created. Rings segment 160/0.20 mm implanted. Bandage contact lens on operative eye and Vigamox drops.
    a. 65767-LT
    b. 65771-LT
    c. 65772-LT
    d. 65770-LT

56. A 3-year-old male with laceration of right upper eyelid scheduled for suturing of eyelid wound. General anesthesia administered. Routine cleaning and draping. Laceration cleaned. 7 interrupted 7-0 vicryl sutures taken to oppose the laceration. Hemostasis achieved. Wound cleaned and covered with steristrip. No blood loss. No postoperative complications.
    a. 67930-E3
    b. 67924-E3
    c. 67935-E3
    d. 67938-E3

57. A patient with left ear tinnitus and labyrinthitis. Vital signs checked and recorded. Examined by Dr. James. Patient consent given for 1st dose of intratympanic injection to the left ear. Injection performed by doctor. Home medication prescribed with instructions. Patient discharged in good condition. CPT code is:
    a. 69801-LT
    b. 69905
    c. 69801
    d. 69905-LT

58. Patients complains of left eye Exotropia. Physician performed strabismus surgery left eye with placement of adjustable sutures. Estimated blood loss 1 ml. Betadinme wash + BSS wash then applied speculum to open the eyelids. Direction fixating suture at 12 o clock with 47/0 silk suture. Left medial conjunctival incision 5 mm from limbus with wisscot. Incision completed to hook left eye medial rectus resection 4 mm from the original incision. Insertion performed using adjustable suture using 6/0 vicryl. Incision performed to hook left lateral rectus resection 6 mm from the original incision. Incision completed using adjustable suture using 6/0 vicryl. Closure of conjunctiva by 8/0 vicryl. Tobradex ointment applied. No complications.
    a. 67311-LT, 67335-LT
    b. 67312-LT, 67335-LT
    c. 67314-LT, 67335-LT
    d. 67316-LT, 67335-LT

59. 51-year-old female with exudative retinopathy right eye scheduled for intravitreal injection of pharmacologic agent. No estimated blood loss. Incision performed at pars plana. Aseptic precaution, right eyelid painted and draped, 0.05 ml of eyelea injected 3.5 mm from limbus. No postoperative complications.
    a. 67028-RT, H35.022
    b. 67030-RT, H35.021
    c. 67028-RT, H35.021
    d. 67030-RT, H35.022

60. 36-years-old male neck pain. Ultrasound neck performed. Result of ultrasound: highly solitary, multilobulated mixed echogenicity nodule with partially irregular margins nodule measuring 12.6x7.8 mm with calcification with increased intra and perilesional vascularity. TIRADS 5. admitted for thyroidectomy with radical neck dissection. Estimated blood loss 15 ml. General anesthesia administered. Kocher incision performed. Left hemithyroidectomy performed with frozen section. Malignant. Skin closure completed. Dietary instructions of clear diet. Observe every hour.
    a. 60252, C73
    b. 60254, C73
    c. 60260, C73
    d. 60260, C73

Evaluation and Management

61. Male patient follow-up with significant nausea, epigastric discomfort. Patient complains of tactile fevers. Patient temperature 96.8. Patient has tachycardia with HR of 107, BP 102/54. Patient oral intake very poor, dizziness upon standing. Patient complains of significant nausea and epigastric discomfort. Patient hydrated aggressively with IV Zofran and IV Pepcid for symptomatic relief. Patient scheduled for hydration and labs.

ROS:	All systems were reviewed.
General Examination:	
General Appearance:	Alert. No acute distress. Well developed. Well-nourished.
Head:	Normocephalic, atraumatic, no scalp lesions.
Eyes:	Pupils equal, round, reactive to light and accommodation, sclera non-icteric, extraocular movement intact (EOMI).
Ears:	Normal, hearing intact to whispered voice.
Nose:	Nares patent, no lesions, septum intact.
Heart:	Regular rate and rhythm, S1, S2 normal, no murmurs, rubs, gallops.
Lungs:	Clear to auscultation bilaterally, no wheezes, rales, rhonchi, B/L Distant breath sounds.
Chest	Normal shape and expansion, LT chest port.
Abdomen:	Bowel sounds present, soft, non-tender, non-distended, no hepatosplenomegaly, no masses palpable.
Back:	Full range of motion, no costovertebral angle tenderness, no kyphosis, no scoliosis, spine nontender to palpation.
Musculoskeletal:	Cervical spine normal, full range of motion, no swelling or deformity.
Skin:	No suspicious lesions, no rashes, no petechia, no ecchymosis.
Neurologic:	Alert and oriented, motor strength normal upper and lower extremities, sensory exam intact, cranial nerves 2-12 grossly intact, gait normal.
PMSH:	Patient is having hypertension and diabetes mellitus.

Assessment:
   1. **Dehydration** - Patient hydrated aggressively. Patient encouraged increasing oral intake of fluids.
   2. **Nausea** - Patient given IV Zofran for symptomatic relief.
   3. **Epigastric discomfort** - Patient given IV Pepcid for epigastric discomfort.
   a. 99214
   b. 99202
   c. 99283
   d. 99284

62. A new patient with history. Examination of EPF and medical decision making straight forward. Patient to go into evaluation and management level.
    a. 99201
    b. 99202
    c. 99203
    d. 99204

63. An elderly patient with respiratory failure with sepsis admitted for critical care. Provider given critical care services for 1 hour 30 minutes. E&M code is:
    a. 99291, 99292, 99292
    b. 99292
    c. 99291
    d. 99291, 99292

64. A comprehensive history and examination and moderate complexity of medical decision making of Initial hospital care.
    a. 99221
    b. 99231
    c. 99222
    d. 99232

65. How many HPI elements required to be extended HPI?
    a. 5
    b. 4
    c. 3
    d. 6

66. No distinction is made between new and established patients in the emergency department.
    a. True
    b. False

67. Male patient at emergency department with right knee pain. Examined. Pain scale 4, radiating to right hip. Patient evaluated, detailed history. Detailed physical exam. Moderate complexity of medical decision making. E & M code is:
    a. 99213
    b. 99202
    c. 99283
    d. 99284

68. A 42-year-old male patient scheduled for follow up. Three lesions on the side of the abdomen for four months. The condition started rapidly on a progressive course, evolving, changing lesion. Highly suspicious of atypical transformation. Erythema swelling and induration, affecting the anterior aspect of the abdomen. Lesion increasing in size with tenderness and discomfort, surrounding irritation, bleeding, redness.
    ROS:

General/Constitutional:	Chills denied, fever denied.
Allergy/Immunology:	Itching present, rash present, sneezing denied.
ENT:	Mouth sores denied. Decreased hearing denied. Sore throat denied.
Respiratory:	Shortness of breath denies, chest pain denies.
Skin:	Erythema present, swelling and induration present.
PFSH:	Right knee replacement June 2016.
Physical Examination:	
General Examination:	Alert in no acute distress, well developed, nourished.
Head:	Normocephalic, atraumatic, no scalp lesion.
Eyes:	Pupils equal, round, reactive to light and accommodation, sclera non-icteric, extraocular movement intact (EOMISkin: a single lesion noted on the anterior aspect of the abdomen, right subcostal area pigment. Irritation is including hyperpigmented globules.
Lungs:	Clear to auscultation bilaterally, no wheezes, rales, rhonchi.
Chest:	Normal shape and expansion; left chest wall and right chest wall post-surgical changes scar, pacemaker LT chest wall.
Female Genitourinary:	Deferred.
Musculoskeletal:	Cervical spine normal, full range of motion, no swelling or deformity.
Extremities:	No clubbing, cyanosis, or edema.
Peripheral Pulses:	2+ throughout, extremities warm.
Podiatric:	Normal.
Psych:	Cognitive function intact, cooperative with exam, judgement, and insight good, anxious.
Diagnosis:	Benign neoplasm of abdomen.

Plan: Excision of biopsy and Topical anti-inflammatory and topical steroids for two weeks.

    a. 99212
    b. 99214
    c. 99204
    d. 99283

69. A patient admitted to hospital for diarrhea and dehydration. IV treatment with normal saline to hydrate the patient. Evaluated day of admission, detailed history, comprehensive examination, low complexity of medical decision making.

    a. 99221
    b. 99223
    c. 99233
    d. 99231

Anesthesia

70. A female 36 weeks gestation scheduled for cesarean delivery. Anesthesia administered at 10:47 ending at 11:35. Routine preparation. Pfannenstiel incision to the skin, abdominal wall opened in layers. Bladder pushed down; lower segment opened transversely. Baby delivered by cephalic forceps, and placenta delivered by continuous cord traction. Uterus closed in one layer, rectus sheath and subcutaneous tissue closed. Skin closed subcuticul. What is the anesthesia code for this procedure?
    a. 01961
    b. 01960
    c. 01962
    d. 01963

71. A 42-year-old male patient scheduled for arthroscopy wrist. Anesthesia administered at 9:10 ending at 10:55. Patient in operating room. Tight forearm prepped and draped. Tourniquet on the right forearm inflated. Arthroscope inserted through the lateral portal followed by instrumentation through the medial portal. Tear debrided and sutured with single PDS. Scapholunate ligament found dorsally deficient and repaired. Below elbow cast for four weeks. Wound closed. Compressive dressing. Patient tolerated surgical procedure. Transferred to recovery room in satisfactory condition. Anesthesia code for this procedure:
    a. 01820
    b. 01810
    c. 01830
    d. 01829

72. Which physical status modifier states "A patient with severe systemic disease?"
    a. P1
    b. P3
    c. P5
    d. P6

73. A 47-year-old patient scheduled for closed reduction of metacarpal fracture. Anesthesia administered from 8:54 to 9:54. Closed reduction performed. Aligned in the form of normal anatomical position for displacement of fracture. Cast applied. Anesthesia code for this procedure:
    a. 01810
    b. 01829
    c. 01832
    d. 01820

74. A 71-year-old patient scheduled for open treatment of patellar fracture with internal fixation for his comminuted fracture of patella with ruptured reinaculum. Prepped and draped. Anesthesiologist administered general anesthesia. Midline incision 10 cm performed on right patella. Comminuted fracture at patella and ruptured retinaculum. Reduction performed with two k-wires. Fixation performed with eight tight band wires and repairing on the retinaculum. Confirmation of articular surface reduction. Drilling performed; 6 mm hole in proximal tibial tuberosity. Suturing and securing with fiber wire stitches. CPT for Anesthesia for:
    a. 01392, 99100
    b. 01390, 99100
    c. 01360, 99116
    d. 01340, 99116

75. A 42-year-old with non-traumatic subarachnoid hemorrhage scheduled for insertion of brain fluid device. Anesthesiologist administered general anesthesia at 4:00 p.m., procedure began at 4:30 p.m. Patient in supine position. Cleaning and draping. Small burr hole performed on the left frontal region over the frontal horn. External ventricular drain inserted, and clear fluid came under pressure. Drain canalized under the skin and connected to external drainage system. Classical closure. Completed surgery at 5:30 p.m. Anesthesiologist releases patient to nurse for postoperative care. No complications. How would you calculate the anesthesia time for this service?
    a. 1hr 15mins
    b. 1hr 00mins
    c. 1hr 30mins
    d. 1hr 45mins

Radiology

76. A 62-year-old female scheduled for exam at OPD orthopedic clinic. Complains of right foot pain of several years, limitation of plantar flexion in the tarsometatarsal joint of the big toe of right foot and dorsiflexion.

    Ordered two view x-rays of the right foot. Advanced degenerating changes. What is the CPT for radiology?
    a. 73615-RT
    b. 73620-RT
    c. 73630-RT
    d. 73650-RT

77. **CT left ankle:**

    Clinical History: Left ankle osteochondritis and talar dome lesion.

    Findings:
    A hypodense lesion at subarticular region of the medial side of the talar dome measuring about 5.6 x 2.6 x 3.6 mm in maximum dimensions. Subtle bulge of overlying articular surface. No definite bony defect or loose body seen.

    Prominence of tapering and projection of the tip of medial malleolus is seen with bulging of the opposing surface of the talus. Calcaneal and tendo-Achilles spurs. No definite fractures. No significant degenerative changes. No bony masses. No soft tissue masses.

    Impression:

    Osteochondral lesion of the medial talar dome as described.
    Calcaneal and tendo-Achilles spurs.
    a. 73702-LT
    b. 73701-LT
    c. 73700-LT
    d. 73706-LT

78. **Indication:** A patient with uterine leiomyoma scheduled for MRI of the pelvis.

    Findings:
    Uterus is retroflexed and enlarged in size, measures 10.6 x 6.8x 7.4 cm. Endometrium measures 13.5 mm. Junctional zone measures 4 mm. Submucosal fibroid measuring 4.5 x 4 x

4 cm; with broad base to the anterior endometrial lining. Right ovary measures 2.3 x 1.5 cm. Right ovary appears normal. Left ovary measures 2.7 x 1.5 cm. No free fluid no in the POD. The rectum appears normal. No evidence of rectal wall thickening. Levator ani and other pelvic floor muscles normal. Visualized pelvic bones and sacrum normal. Visualized lumbar spine normal.

Impression: Bulky fibroid uterus.

   a. 72195
   b. 72196
   c. 72197
   d. 72198

79. **Ultrasound Neck:**
    Clinical Details: Parathyroid adenoma.
    Findings:
    Isthmus measures 2 mm. Right thyroid lobe measures 35.6 x 22.2 x 16.1 mm with a volume of 6.7 cc. Left thyroid lobe measures 36.3 x 24.6 x 14.6 mm with a volume of 6.8 cc with a solitary left mid polar well circumscribed. Hypo to isoechoic nodule measuring 8.2 x 7.3 mm with a few echogenic specks.

    Right neck lymph node at level III measuring 12.3 x 3.8 mm.
    Right neck lymph node at level II measuring 13.3 x 4.1 mm. Left neck lymph node at level III measuring 10.9 x 3.8 mm. Left neck lymph node at level II measuring 8.6 x 4.6 mm. Solitary right superior posterior adenoma measuring 6.1 x 4.4 mm.
    Opinion:
    Solitary right superior posterior adenoma measuring 6.1 x 4.4 mm. Solitary left mid polar well-circumscribed hypo to isoechoic nodule measuring 8.2 x 7.3 mm with a few echogenic specks -TIRADS 3. Bilateral nonspecific cervical lymphadenopathy.
    a. 76529
    b. 76604
    c. 76536
    d. 76641

80. **Hrct Thorax:**
    Clinical History: COVID infection
    Technique: HRCT imaging was performed with sub-millimeter scan of thorax from the level of thoracic inlet to the diaphragm. Mediastinal soft tissue window acquired.

    Findings:
    Focal consolidation seen peripherally in posterior basal segment of right lung measuring 5.4mm. Subtle ground glass opacity seen in left upper lobe measuring 2.2mm. Both lungs show normal aeration and inflation. The hilar region on each side is unremarkable, and the main bronchi appear normal. Mediastinal soft tissue characterization would require contrast study evaluation. No evident pleural / pericardial effusion is seen. The thoracic skeleton and thoracic soft tissues show no abnormalities.

    Comments:
    Focal consolidation peripherally in posterior basal segment of right lung measuring 5.4mm. Subtle ground glass opacity left upper lobe measuring 2.2mm.
    These are nonspecific findings which can be seen in early COVID or non-COVID pathologies and needs correlation with clinical profile.
    a. 71260
    b. 71250
    c. 71270
    d. 71275

81. **Examination:** Routine MRI of the right knee was performed without contrast.

    Findings:

    Grossly intact medial and lateral tibiofemoral articulations together with the intervening chondral cartilage showing no obvious signs of tibiofemoral osteoarthritis or gross osteochondral lesions. The small previously seen focal osteochondral injury related to the posterior medial corner of the medial femoral condyle deep of the femoral attachment of the medial head of gastrocnemius has remarkably resolved together with the surrounding bone marrow edema. Sprain of the posterolateral bundle of the anterior cruciate ligament, otherwise the ligament appears grossly intact in the dedicated coronal oblique sequences. Signs of patella alta with long undulated course of the patellar tendon, otherwise it appears intact. Intact quadriceps tendon. No Baker's cyst formation. Small amount of joint effusion with infrapatellar fat impingement more obvious toward the inferior pole of the patella which shows focal irregularity and mild bone marrow oedema. Mild changes of popliteal tenosynovitis with intact patellar tendon.

    Conclusion:
    Patella Alta with shallow femoral trochlea and severe grade IV hanges of hondromalacia patellae showing no changes in comparison to the previous study. Significant resolution of

small osteochondral injury of the posterior medial femoral condyle. Small amount of joint effusion with infrapatellar fat impingement, signs of synovitis.
   a. 73720-RT
   b. 73719-RT
   c. 73718-RT
   d. 73721-RT

82. X-Ray of Lumbosacral Spine-AP/Lateral View.

   Clinical Details: Low Back Pain.
   Findings:
   Mild tilting of lumbar spine. Mild reduced disc space at L4-L5 and L5-S1 Levels. The lumbar vertebrae show normal height, density and alignment. No evidence of spondylolysis or spondylolisthesis. Rest of the intervertebral disc heights maintained. Posterior arch elements normal. Pre and para vertebral soft tissues normal.
   Impression:
   Normal x-ray of lumbosacral spine.
   a. 72100, M54.5
   b. 72110, M54.5
   c. 72114, M54.5
   d. 72080, M54.5

83. **Abdominal Ultrasound**

   Clinical History: Epigastric pain

   Findings:
   The liver is normal in size measures 14 cm, homogeneous echotexture focal.
   Hypoechoic texture within the right lobe, measured 10x7 mm reveals hemangioma.
   Normal gallbladder, well distended of normal wall thickness, no stones or sludge, no pericholecystic fluid collection.
   CBD and portal vein are of normal caliber.
   Pancreas normal in size & texture.
   Spleen measures 7.9 cm, normal in size and texture.
   IVC & aorta unremarkable.
   Right kidney measures about 10 x 3.6 cm.
   Left kidney measures about 9.1 x 4.2 cm.
   Both kidneys normal in size, smooth in outline showing normal cortical thickness and echogenicity, no stones or hydronephrosis.
   No free fluid or collection.

Impression:
Right liver lobe hemangioma

    a. 76705
    b. 76706
    c. 76700
    d. 76775

84. **Clinical indication:** 3-month follow-up ultrasound. History of lymphoma. Family history of breast cancer in mother in her 70s.

    Technical Factors: Real-time scan of the left breast was performed.
    Finding:
    Left breast: There is a benign-appearing wider than tall solid mass at 3.30 positions left breast, 4 cm from the nipple. Measures 2.3 x 0.7 x 1.8 cm with no internal color flow or posterior shadowing. Stable.
    Impression: Stable probable benign mass at 3.30 left breast. Continued sonographic follow-up would be recommended in 6 months to confirm stability.
    BI-RADS: 3 – Probably Benign.
    Recommendation:
    Follow up in 6 months.
        a. 76645, N63.20
        b. 76882, N63.20
        c. 76445, N63.10
        d. 76882, N63.10

Laboratory/Pathology

85. A 61-year-old male scheduled for deep venous thrombosis of lower extremities. Full hypercoagulation workup performed. Coumadin therapy, 3 mg daily. Labs Prothrombin Time performed. Follow up after three weeks, routine examination.
    a. 85730
    b. 85610
    c. 85611
    d. 85612

86. A male with mild anemia, iron panel results of 12.9. CPT code for iron panel is:
    a. 83582
    b. 83570
    c. 83550
    d. 83540

87. Patient scheduled for complete blood count. CBC with hemoglobin 14.0, hematocrit 40.6, RBC 4.97, platelets of 357, and WBC with 8.7. Results within normal limits. What is the pathology code for CBC?
    a. 85032
    b. 85018
    c. 85025
    d. 85041

88. A patient with significant abdominal pain and GERD. Patient's abdominal pain located upper left quadrant and epigastric region. Lipase evaluation ordered. Treatment after lab results.

    a. 83690
    b. 83695
    c. 83698
    d. 83700

89. A patient with Vitamin D deficiency scheduled for Vitamin D, 25 Hydroxy Labs. Results 41, normal limits. CPT code for the Lab test?
    a. 82310
    b. 82306
    c. 82300
    d. 82308

90. Which of the below test is not included in renal function panel?
    a. Carbon dioxide
    b. Potassium
    c. Albumin
    d. IgM antibody

91. The patient in excellent health. Longstanding history of hypertension, and diabetes. Patient developed significant tachycardia, significant dizziness, and nausea. Basic metabolic panel ordered. Results; CO_2 30, BUN 24, sodium 135, potassium 5.0, chloride 102, glucose 127, urea nitrogen 19 creatinine 0.8, and calcium 10.2. All normal limits except glucose 127. Normal range of glucose is 74-100. Patient's glucose slightly high with 127. Lab results discussed; dietary management education provided.
    a. 85025
    b. 80048
    c. 80047
    d. 80050

92. 38-year-old with increased heart rate and anxiety. Two-day history of palpitation and slight SOB. No sweating or shaky hands. No change in bowel habit. Patient examined. Thyroid Stimulating Hormone ordered. TSH performed. Results within normal limits.
    a. 84442
    b. 84445
    c. 84446
    d. 84443

93. What is the correct coding for hepatic function panel with Albumin, Bilirubin total, Bilirubin direct, phosphatase alkaline, and protein?
    a. 80076
    b. 80076, 82040, 82247, 82248, 84075
    c. 82040, 82247, 82248, 84075, 84155
    d. 82040, 82247, 82248, 84460, 84450

Medicine

94. **Clinical History:** Left foot ischemia.
    Remarks: Request for lower limb venous doppler study.
    Findings:
    On B mode scan the diffuse atherosclerotic wall thickening with multifocal small calcified plaques involving left external iliac artery, common femoral artery and superficial femoral artery. Echogenic thrombus involving distal part of left superficial femoral and popliteal artery extending to anterior tibial, posterior tibial, and peroneal artery. Distal part of anterior tibial, posterior tibial, and dorsalis pedis artery is not well-evaluated due to overlying soft tissue edema.
    On color flow and pulse wave analysis patchy intermittent color flow with low-velocity biphasic flow wave pattern involving left common femoral and proximal superficial femoral artery. No evidence of color filling or appreciable flow involving distal part of left superficial femoral, popliteal artery, and evaluated anterior tibial, posterior tibial, and peroneal artery. No obvious aneurysm or AV malformation involving evaluated arterial tree.

    Conclusion:
    Thrombosis of left distal superficial femoral and popliteal artery extending to anterior tibial, posterior tibial, and peroneal artery. Compromised flow wave pattern involving left common femoral and proximal superficial femoral artery. Diffuse atherosclerotic wall thickening with multifocal small calcified atheromatous plaques involving left external iliac artery, common femoral artery, and superficial femoral artery. What is the code?
    a. 93976-LT
    b. 93975-LT
    c. 93970-LT
    d. 93971-LT

95. Patient with dehydration and poor intake of fluids. Patient reports not liking/wanting to drink water. Importance of staying hydrated emphasized. Administered normal saline 500 ml. Two hours started at 9:30 a.m. to 11:30 a.m. Patient reports feeling better with hydration therapy. What is the CPT for this service?
    a. 96360
    b. 96360, 96361
    c. 96361
    d. 96361, 96361

96. A 65-year-old female with malignant neoplasm of ovary, stage IV. Scheduled for administration of chemotherapy agent Avastin. Avastin administered intravenously for one hour, started at 4:00 p.m. to 5:00 p.m.
    a. 96401
    b. 96402
    c. 96415
    d. 96413

97. **Indication:**   Carpal tunnel syndrome.
    Test: Motor and Nerve conduction study.
    Findings:
    Motor conduction study from bilateral median nerves revealed prolonged distal latencies. Sensory conduction study from bilateral median nerves revealed prolonged peak latencies. Reduction in SNAPs from right median nerve compared to left side. The motor and sensory conduction study from bilateral ulnar nerves revealed latencies and amplitudes. F-waves revealed normal latencies from all the nerves tested.

    Conclusion:
    The nerve conduction study revealed moderate degree of carpal tunnel syndrome on both sides.
    a. 95903
    b. 95904
    c. 95905
    d. 95908

98. A 57-year-old male admitted to ICU with bilateral pneumonia with respiratory failure. On ventilator for first day. Sedated with morphine and midazolam infusions on PC. PC: 22, PEEP: 6, RR: 32, FIO2: 50%, SPO2: 96%. Hemodynamically stable. HR: 88/min, BP: 130/72, Chest: Reduced air entry at both bases bilaterally. Code for ventilator services?
    a. 94002
    b. 94003
    c. 94004
    d. 94005

99. A one-year-old patient scheduled for Hepatitis A vaccine. Patient prepped. Administered Hepatitis A vaccine intramuscularly. Counseling given to parent, i.e. safety and health precautions. Code this vaccination services.
    a. 90461
    b. 90471
    c. 90472
    d. 90460

100. A 19-years-old patient in emergency department with diarrhea. No fever or vomiting. Mild abdominal cramping with eating. Nausea present. Patient examined by the physician. Inserted IV cannula. Viasol 40mg IV started at 4:00 p.m. ended at 5:00 p.m. Zofran 4 mg, IV in normal saline given as a push. At 6:00 p.m. hooked ringer lactate to run for one hour, stopped at 7:00 p.m. What are the Infusion codes?
    a. 96374, 96375, 96361
    b. 96360, 96375, 96365
    c. 96365, 96366, 96361
    d. 96365, 96375, 96361

101. An 86-year-old patient with ESRD scheduled for hemodialysis. Patient to remain in ICU for hemodynamics, neurological monitoring, and hemodialysis. Hemodialysis scheduled. Patient is still with high creatinine with 917 ug/ml. administered all blood transfusions via the arterial port in the dialysis blood circuit. Transfused for total 30 minutes. Patient is to continue DVT prophylaxis. Patient fully conscious and hemodynamically stable. What is the CPT for this service?

    a. 90935, 99213-25
    b. 90935
    c. 90937, 99213-25
    d. 90937

102. A 19-year-old patient with generalized tonic-clonic seizure. Patient takes Keppra 500 mg. Urgent EEG awake and drowsy performed. Awake; 10 Hz alpha rhythm of 50 uV -- symmetric and reactive to eye-opening. Drowsiness. Deeper stages of sleep are not achieved. Abnormality in EEG; three bursts of rhythms, frontal delta, left greater than right. Two occur in wakefulness and one in drowsiness. Hyperventilation did not activate the record. Photic stimulation did not activate the record.

    Impression: Abnormal EEG due to three bursts of asymmetric, rhythmic frontal delta, left greater than right without obvious spikes.
    a. 95819
    b. 95822
    c. 95812
    d. 95816

Medical Terminology

103. To remove a portion or suspicious tissue for pathologic examination:
    a. Removal
    b. Excision
    c. Biopsy
    d. Repair

104. Hemostasis is:
    a. The stoppage of blood flow.
    b. Bleeding under the skin due to trauma
    c. Redness of the skin or mucous membrane
    d. Protein in red blood cells

105. Closer to the back of the body or a structure:
    a. Lateral
    b. Medial
    c. Anterior
    d. Posterior

106. Oximetry is:
    a. Measurement of the level of oxygen in the blood
    b. Measurement of the level of the blood
    c. Measurement of the level of the air in lungs
    d. Measurement of the size of the lungs

107. An artificial device that replaces a body part is:
    a. Stent
    b. Catheter
    c. Prosthesis
    d. Pacemaker

108. Retractor is:
    a. Surgical instrument used to retract wound edges or deeper tissues
    b. Surgical instrument used to free up organs
    c. Surgical instrument used to close small incisions
    d. Surgical instrument used to separate tissue layers

109. What is the meaning of prefix eu-?

a. Outside, beyond
b. Bad, painful
c. Good, normal
d. Equal, same

110. The position of face down or palm down is called:
    a. Prone
    b. Supine
    c. Coronal
    d. Sagittal

111. What is the number of Hex-?
    a. Three
    b. One
    c. Four
    d. Six

Anatomy

112. Lateral compartment is:
    a. One of the three joint compartments in the hand
    b. One of the three joint compartments in the knee
    c. One of the three joint compartments in the metatarsals
    d. One of the three joint compartments in the metacarpals

113. Transparent anterior part of the eyeball:
    a. Iris
    b. Eye
    c. Cornea
    d. Pupil

114. What is bile?
    a. A substance produced in the liver
    b. A substance produced in the kidney
    c. A substance produced in the stomach
    d. A substance produced in the esophagus

115. The digestive tract from the pylorus, the opening at the bottom of the stomach all the way the anus.
    a. Epidermis
    b. Lungs
    c. Arteries
    d. Intestines

116. The scrotum is:
    a. The sac that contains the testes, or testicles
    b. Which carry the blood away from the heart
    c. System of tubes that carries air
    d. Which protect against germs and microorganisms

117. Bone in the upper arm:
    a. Femur
    b. Radius
    c. Tibia
    d. Humerus

118. Layers of the skin are:
    a. Epidermis, Dermis, subcutaneous tissue
    b. Connective tissue, hair follicles, sweat glands
    c. Hair follicles, Dermis, Connective tissue
    d. Epidermis, sweat glands, hair follicles

119. How many vertebral segments spinal cord has?
    a. 28
    b. 30
    c. 26
    d. 31

120. Uterine artery is a branch of:
    a. Common iliac artery
    b. External iliac artery
    c. Internal iliac artery
    d. Descending aorta

ICD-10-CM/Diagnosis

121. A 20-year-old male with acute abdominal pain, nausea, and anorexia. Condition started with abdominal pain in the epigastric region, shifted to the right lower quadrant, progressive. Associated symptoms, diarrhea, vomiting, and nausea. Abdominal examination showed tender right iliac fossa with rebound tenderness. Labs performed: WBCS 10.72, Neut 78.7, CRP 77.1. CT scan performed. Retrocecal appendix 9.2 mm with solitary appendicolith measuring 6.7 mm with peri-appendiceal dirty fat stranding.
    Diagnosis: Acute appendicitis. Laparoscopic appendectomy scheduled. ICD 10 code is:
    a. K35.31
    b. K35.32
    c. K35.33
    d. K35.80

122. A 52-year-old female patient with swelling and pain in neck for six months. Ultrasound ordered. The clinical palpable lump at the right side of the neck is a subcutaneous nodule, 3 cm lipoma at the neck.
    Diagnosis: Lipoma of neck. Treatment options discussed.
    a. R22.1
    b. D17.0
    c. R22.0
    d. D17.39

123. A 29-year-old male with chronic right wrist pain. Pain increases with activities, i.e. extension, flexion, more so during sports activities. Examination revealed swelling over the dorsal aspect of right wrist. X-ray and MRI were performed. Evidence of ganglion of right wrist. As the patient is in pain despite trial of rest and medications and surgical excision of the ganglion of the right wrist.
    a. M67.431
    b. M67.432
    c. M67.421
    d. M67.422

124. ICD-10 for Capillary hemangioma of intracranial region is:
    a. D18.01
    b. D18.09
    c. D18.03
    d. D18.02

125. A female with fever, flank pain, and burning urination. Urinalysis and imaging test performed. Diagnosis is chronic obstructive pyelonephritis. Treatment options discussed, and medications given.
   a. N11.1
   b. N13.2
   c. N11.8
   d. N11.0

126. ICD-10 code for acute gonococcal salpingo-oophoritis is:
   a. N70.03
   b. O08.0
   c. A54.24
   d. N70.93

127. A 38-year-old male with recurrent attacks of biliary colics. Tender right hypochondriac point. Ultrasound revealed acute cholecystitis. Surgical intervention and other treatment options were discussed. Elected for laparoscopic cholecystectomy. Scheduled. ICD-10 code is:
   a. K81.1
   b. K81.0
   c. K81
   d. K80.81

128. A 60-year-old male with longstanding history of elevated PSA. Significant back pain. CT scan pelvic region. Evidence of prostate cancer. PSA raised to 407.10H. Case discussed in detail, and patient to continue with low dose weekly toxol. Consideration of clinical trials will be made if, at any point, the patient progresses through chemotherapy. ICD-10 code for Prostate cancer is:
   a. C61
   b. C60.9, R97.21
   c. R97.21
   d. C61, R97.21

129. A 48-year-old female diagnosed with malignant neoplasm of central portion of right female breast in October 2019. Scheduled for chemotherapy. Saggy breasts: upper pole is concave on both sides. No skin fixity. Pectoral muscle is well defined, 50% of breast outside the footprint of muscle. Thin lower abdominal tissue. Excellent metabolic response to chemotherapy with reduction right breast lesions. No diabetes. No HTN. No allergies. Hypothyroidism. ICD codes and sequencing for this patient are:
    a. Z51.11, C50.111, E03.9
    b. E03.9, C50.111, Z51.11
    c. C50.111, E03.9
    d. C50.111, Z51.11

130. A 62-year-old patient scheduled for management of CKD-4. Has diabetes mellitus and HTN. Fully conscious and oriented. HR: 72 bpm. Chest: Clear. CVS: Normal S1, S2. No added sounds. Abdomen: Distended, soft. Bowel sounds audible. No hydronephrosis, no calculus disease. Both kidneys are relatively enlarged with normal parenchymal echo pattern. Final diagnosis is Chronic Kidney Disease Four, diabetes mellitus, and hypertension.
    a. N18.4, I10, E11.9
    b. N18.4, I13.9, E11.22
    c. N18.4, I12.9, E11.9
    d. N18.4, I12.9, E11.22

131. A 30-year-old female, gravida 3, para 2+0, at OPD clinic with history of 34 weeks gestation. Patient on insulin since 1st trimester of pregnancy. Blood sugars are at present controlled on Novorapid 18 units at breakfast, 10 units each at lunch and dinner. Patient had emergency cesarean section six years ago for failure to progress due to cephalopelvic disproportion at 2nd stage of labor. Patient is advised elective LSCS under spinal anesthesia at 38 weeks. High risk for stillbirth due to high doses of insulin. Needs delivery by 38 weeks of gestation. Correct ICD-10 codes are?
    a. O24.414, Z3A.34, Z79.4
    b. O24.414, Z3A.38, Z79.4
    c. O24.415, Z3A.34, Z79.4
    d. O24.416, Z3A.38, Z79.4

132. Referral patient for a second opinion at orthopedic clinic. Severe pain and swelling of right knee due to an old injury. Clinical examination of right knee revealed severe pain on stressing the patellofemoral joint with positive McMurray's test suggestive of torn medial meniscus. An MRI scan of the right knee has confirmed grade II tear of the posterior horn both medial and lateral meniscus. Final diagnosis is tear of posterior horn of medial and lateral meniscus. Recommended to resolve severe right knee condition to perform arthroscopic surgery.
    a. M23.221, M23.252
    b. M23.222, M23.252
    c. M23.221, M23.251
    d. M25.561, M25.461

HCPCS Level II

133. HCPCS Level II code for Prednisolone, oral, 5mg is:
    a. J7510
    b. J7502
    c. J7512
    d. J7505

134. Patient with case of end-stage renal disease scheduled for renal dialysis. Procedure performed by Dialysis access system (Implantable). HCPCS II code is:
    a. C2621
    b. C1887
    c. C1881
    d. C2615

135. Patient suffering with vomiting and nausea. Infusion drug ondansetron 4 mg administered in 100 ml normal saline. HCPCS Level II code for infusion therapy is:
    a. Q0163
    b. Q0081
    c. Q0092
    d. Q0169

136. Patient in an accident arrived via emergency transport ambulance service for basic life support. HCPCS Level code is:
    a. A0429
    b. A0431
    c. A0888
    d. A0435

137. After complete antiseptic measures and patient in supine position. Right thumb exposed. Lacerated deep wound on the volar aspect of the right thumb. Wound exploration performed. Superficial tear of tendon sheath. Debridement lacerated tissues and suturing. Dressing. Thumb spica splint applied. Select correct option for HCPCS level II code for thumb spica splint:
    a. L3908, F5
    b. L3807, F5
    c. L3809, F5
    d. L3908, F5

138. Patient scheduled for immediate breast reconstruction with breast prosthesis implant due to right breast cancer. General anesthesia administered. Implantation performed with breast prosthesis of silicone material. The HCPCS level II code for breast prosthesis is:
    a. L8030, RT
    b. L8032, RT
    c. L8035, RT
    d. L8040, RT

Coding guidelines

139. As per coding convention what is meaning of the word "AND," when it appears in a title:
    a. Only And
    b. "And" or "Or"
    c. Only Or
    d. And & And

140. When a related definitive diagnosis not established by provider signs and symptoms are not acceptable for reporting purposes.
    a. True
    b. False

141. What is the sequencing when both acute and chronic codes documented and both codes are present for that diagnosis?
    a. Acute only
    b. Chronic Only
    c. Chronic code first following Acute code
    d. Acute code first following Chronic code

142. When type of diabetes is not mentioned in the medical record the default code is:
    a. E11.9-Type II diabetes without complications
    b. E10.9-Type 1 diabetes without complications
    c. Both Type 1 diabetes and Type II diabetes
    d. No code should be coded

143. As per the official ICD-10 guidelines, postpartum begins .... and continues till .... weeks following delivery.
    a. After one day, seven weeks
    b. After two days, five weeks
    c. Before one day, eight weeks
    d. Immediately, six weeks

144. ICD-10 guidelines say if no bilateral code is provided and the condition is bilateral, assign unspecified laterality codes for both the left and right side.
    a. True
    b. False

Compliance and Regulatory

145. What are the identifying codes and terminology purpose of the CPT?
     a. To give numbers in the medical records
     b. To provide uniform language among physicians, patients, and third parties
     c. For collecting the money from patients and third parties
     d. To file the medical records at the hospitals and third parties

146. Non-face-to-face services, telephonic and online services are valid coding services:
     a. Yes
     b. No

147. The effective date for the use of the updated CPT code set is:
     a. April 1st
     b. January 1st
     c. May 1st
     d. October 1st

148. It is not recognized the services or procedures performed by the providers that are not found in the CPT code set:
     a. True
     b. False

149. The CPT code set was designated by the Department of Health and Human Services as the national coding standard for physicians and other health care professional services and procedures is under which act?
     a. WHO
     b. OIG
     c. HIPAA
     d. AMA

150. The correct statement is for add-on codes; they are always performed in addition to the primary service or procedure and must never be reported as a stand-alone code.
     a. Yes
     b. No

ANSWER KEY - PRACTICE TEST #2

10,000 Series

1. **Answer: A**
   10060 incision and drainage of abscess simple or single is the appropriate code for this procedure. Since it is not multiple or complicated 10060 simple or single incisions and drainage of the abscess is coded.

2. **Answer C**
   11043 debridement, muscle, or fascia, first 20 sq cm or less is the appropriate code for this procedure. Provider did debridement for patient's complaint for grade for bed sores since patient is suffering with it.

3. **Answer: A**
   11406 excision, benign lesion including margins, except skin tag, trunk, arms, or legs; excised diameter over 4.0 cm is the right code for this procedure. Since patient's lesion size is 8.9 cm took this code of diameter over 4.0 cm.

4. **Answer: B**
   10021 fine needle aspiration biopsy, without imaging guidance, first lesion is the appropriate code for this procedure. Physician performed FNA biopsy for analysis of the lesion to check the malignancy without any ultrasound guidance or fluoroscopic guidance.

5. **Answer: D**
   12001 simple repair of superficial wounds of scalp, axillae, external genitalia, trunk and/or extremities (including hands and feet); 2.5 cm or less. For patient's skin cut on the left-hand finger physician performed closure of the cut through simple repair. 12001 is the code for 2.5 cm or less size of the wound and patient's wound size is less than 2 cm.

6. **Answer: C**
   19120 excision of cyst, fibroadenoma, or other benign or malignant tumor, aberrant breast tissue, duct lesion, nipple, or areola lesion, open, male or female, 1 or more lesions is the appropriate code for this procedure. As patient is suffering with malignant neoplasm of nipple and areola physician treated the patient with surgical intervention with removing the

lesion of the breast. RT for Laterality used to identify procedures performed on the right side of the body.

7. **Answer: B**
   11402 excision, benign lesion including margins, except skin tags, trunk, arms or legs, excised diameter 1.1 to 2.0 cm is for submammary lesion measuring 2 cm. 11420- Excision, benign lesion including margins, except skin tags, scalp, neck, hands, feet, genitalia excised diameter 0.5 cm or less for neck lesion measuring 0.5 cm with 59 modifier distinct procedural service. Modifier 59 is to identify a procedure, which is distinct and independent service from other procedure that the provider performs on the same day. Simple repair is not required to code for this procedure which is included in the excision as per the CPT coding guidelines for this procedure.

8. **Answer: C**
   11042 debridement, subcutaneous tissue (includes epidermis and dermis, if performed), first 20 sq. cm or less is right answer. Laterality described with modifier RT. Diabetic foot ulcer ICD-10 codes are E11.621, Type II diabetes mellitus with foot ulcer followed by L97.519 Non-pressure chronic ulcer of other part of right foot with unspecified severity.

9. **Answer: A**
   11960 insertion of tissue expander(s) for other than breast, including subsequent expansion for tissue expanders insertion for patient's condition scar and 15770 graft; derma-fat-fascia for the harvesting of fat from abdomen. Fibrosis debridement is included in the primary procedures, which is no need to code separately.

20,000 Series

10. **Answer: B**
    21337, closed treatment of nasal septal fracture and S02.2XXA fracture of nasal bones, initial encounter for closed fracture is correct. Open treatment not performed since it is not open fracture. Since fracture is for initial encounter and not subsequent ICD code S02.2XXA is the correct code.

11. **Answer: A**
    25685 open treatment of trans-scaphoperilunar type of fracture dislocation is the right answer for this procedure. Since the procedure is open procedure and internal fixations done it should be coded as open treatment of the fracture. RT for Laterality used to identify procedures performed on the right side of the body.

12. **Answer: C**
    28238 reconstruction, posterior tibial tendon with excision of accessory tarsal navicular bone is the right code for this procedure. Physician done this procedure for patient's complaints of extra bone or piece of cartilage located in the foot. RT for Laterality used to identify procedures performed on the right side of the body.

13. **Answer: A**
    20680 removal of implant, deep is the correct code for the above procedure. Once the defect healed, the provider removes the implant. LT is for Laterality, used to identify procedures performed on the right side of the body.

14. **Answer: B**
    21555 Excision, tumor, soft tissue of neck or anterior neck, subcutaneously is the right code for this procedure. Patient lesion is subcutaneous and the code 21555 is the code procedure for subcutaneous lesions. Provide removed an abnormal growth from just below the surface of the skin in the neck.

15. **Answer: C**
    27590 amputation, thigh, through femur, any level is the appropriate code for this procedure. In this procedure the provider completely removes the leg at any point on the femur bone of the thigh. Patient is coming for this procedure, physician amputated thigh of the patient.

16. **Answer: B**
    23485 -- osteotomy, clavicle, with or without internal fixation; with bone graft for nonunion or malunion is the right answer. Osteotomy procedure performs on the patient for patient's complaints with internal fixation and the bone graft. Closure is included in the primary procedure, which is no need to code separately. Laterality mentioned with the RT modifier.

17. **Answer: A**
    20680 -- removal of implant; deep (e.g., buried wire, pin, screw, metal band, nail, rod or plate) is the correct answer as physician went into deep structure to remove the implantation. Fracture is a follow up, so coded with S62.667D Nondisplaced fracture of distal phalanx of the left little finger, subsequent encounter for fracture with routine healing. Modifier for the little finger is F4, which is to tell the location of the hand.

18. **Answer: C**
    29882 -- arthroscopy, knee, surgical; with meniscus repair (medial or lateral) is right code with 20902-bone graft, any donor area; major or large. Physician performed arthroscopic chondroplasty, with meniscus repair. Meniscus repair is included in the arthroscopy. Modifier 59 is to identify a procedure, which is distinct and independent service from other procedure that the provider performs on the same day. Laterality described with modifier LT.

30,000 Series

19. **Answer: D**

    31541 -- laryngoscopy with excision of tumor and/or strapping of vocal cords or epiglottis; with operating microscope or telescope is the correct answer for this procedure. The method microscope and excision of the vocal cord lesions are included in this service.

20. **Answer: A**

    36478 -- endovenous ablation therapy of vein, extremity, inclusive of all imaging guidance and monitoring, laser, first vein and 37765 stab phlebectomy of varicose veins, 1 extremity is the right codes for this procedure. For patients' complaints physician ablated and destroyed the wall of diseased vein in an extremity. LT for Laterality used to identify procedures performed on the right side of the body. 59 modifier is to say the second procedure is separate and different procedure from the first procedure.

21. **Answer: C**

    36561 -- insertion of tunneled centrally venous access device, with subcutaneous port; age 5 years or old, 77001 Fluroscopic guidance for central venous access device placement and 76937 ultrasound guidance for vascular access requiring ultrasound evaluation of potential access sites are the appropriate codes for the above procedure. Physician performed central venous access port placement under fluoroscopic guidance and ultrasound guidance. Intubation should not be coded separately as it is included in the procedure.

22. **Answer: A**

    36821 -- anteriovenous anastomosis, open, direct, any site is the right code for this procedure. Provider creates an anteriovenous (AV) anastomosis by connecting a vein to an artery to provide better vascular access in a patient with kidney failure who will receive hemodialysis treatments.

23. **Answer: B**

    36471 -- injection of sclerosant; multiple incompetent veins, same leg. Since solution injected into multiple veins picked 36471 with multiple incompetent veins. This procedure performed to treat vascular malformation of the patient.

24. **Answer: A**

    31600 -- tracheostomy, planned is the right code for this procedure. Since patient is suffering with respiratory failure with sepsis physician performed tracheostomy and exposes the trachea and creates an opening in the windpipe. This code represents planned tracheostomy.

25. **Answer: D**
36475 -- endovenous ablation therapy of incompetent vein, extremity inclusive of all imaging guidance and monitoring, percutaneous radiofrequency, fist vein treated is the code for ablation of the vein with radiofrequency. And for phlebectomy 37765-Stab phlebectomy of varicose veins, 1 extremity;10-20 stab incisions are the correct code as phlebectomy done with 18 stab incisions. Modifier 59 is to identify a procedure, which is distinct and independent service from other procedure that the provider performs on the same day. Laterality described with modifier RT.

26. **Answer: A**
Repair of nasal septum is 30520 -- septoplasty or submucous resection, with or without cartilage scoring, contouring or replacement with graft. Physician reshapes the nasal septum, correcting airway obstruction in above procedure. 30140-Submucous resection inferior turbinate, partial or complete, any method done on both sides of inferior turbinate's, coded 30140 should code twice for the above procedure.

27. **Answer: C**
38510 -- biopsy or excision of lymph node(s); open, deep cervical node(s) is the correct answer. Physician removed cervical lymph nodes, as per the patient's complaints. Repair of incision is not to be coded separately as it is included in the 38510.

40,000 Series

28. **Answer: A**
   46200 -- fissurectomy, including sphincterotomy and 45300 proctosigmoidoscopy, rigid, diagnostic are the correct codes for this procedure. Physician performed fissurectomy including sphincterotomy and rigid proctosimoidoscopy. Need to code 46200 and 45300 as two procedures performed during one encounter. 59 modifier is to indicate that 45300 is separate procedure and need to get reimbursement.

29. **Answer: B**
   46947 -- hemorrhoidopexy by stapling is the right code for this procedure. Provider surgically removed an abnormally enlarged hemorrhoidal tissue, then repositioned the remaining hemorrhoidal tissue back to its normal position and staples the tissue in place for patient's complaints.

30. **Answer: A**
   45172 -- excision of rectal tumor, transanal approach; including muscularis propia full thickness is the appropriate code for this procedure. As patient is suffering with polyp at the anorectal junction provider performed this procedure using a transanal approach, through the anus, and the excised the anorectal polyp.

31. **Answer: A**
   42826 -- tonsillectomy, primary or secondary, age 12 or over is the right code for this procedure. The provider performs a tonsillectomy procedure in a patient who is over 12 years of age or older.

32. **Answer: C**
   49561 -- repair initial incisional or ventral hernia; incarcerated or strangulated and 49568 Implantation of mesh or other prosthesis for open incisional or ventral hernia repair are the right codes for the above procedure. As patient is suffering with Incisional ventral hernia, physician surgically repaired an initial incisional ventral hernia.

33. **Answer: A**
   47562 -- laparoscopy, surgical; cholecystectomy is the right code for the above procedure. The provider removed the gallbladder through a laparoscope to treat gallbladder disease.

34. **Answer: A**
   Physician removed inflamed appendix with laparoscopic method appendectomy, which is

44970 -- laparoscopy, surgical; appendectomy. K35.80 is for unspecified acute appendicitis where patient diagnosed for her complaints.

35. **Answer: B**

    The physician performed flexible colonoscopy and obtained tissue sample. Physician did not used any snare or hot biopsy techniques, did not controlled bleeding or ablated tumor or polyps. 45380 -- colonoscopy, flexible, proximal to splenic flexure; with biopsy single or multiple is the correct code for this procedure.

36. **Answer: A**

    Hemorrhoidectomy performed without any fissurectomy or with fistulectomy, including fissurectomy. 46260 -- hemorrhoidectomy, internal and external, 2 or more columns/groups is the right answer for this procedure. For patient's anal polyp physician performed 46922- destruction of lesion(s), anus, simple, surgical excision done as a simple procedure without cryosurgery or laser surgery. Modifier 59 is to identify a procedure that is distinct and independent from other procedure that the provider performs on the same day. Simple repair is not required for this procedure which is included in the excision as per the CPT coding guidelines for this procedure.

50,000 Series

37. **Answer: B**
    57522 -- conization of cervix, with or without fulguration, with or without dilation and curettage; loop electrode excision is the answer for above procedure. Conization, dilation and curettage performed in loop electrode excision method.

38. **Answer: C**
    54640.2 -- orchiopexy, inguinal or scrotal approach is the right code for this procedure. Physician performed procedure by inguinal approach this procedure coded by 54640. This code coded twice as it is performed on bilateral testicles. RT & LT for Laterality used to identify procedures performed on the right side of the body.

39. **Answer: D**
    55700 -- biopsy, needle or punch, single or multiple, any approach is the right code for this procedure. As patient is suffering with enlarged prostate physician performed biopsy of the prostate gland to test for any abnormal cell growth or cancer.

40. **Answer: B**
    58662 -- laparoscopy, surgical, with fulguration or excision of lesions of the ovary, pelvic viscera, or peritoneal surface by any method is the appropriate code for this procedure. As patient is suffering with chronic salpingitis physician performed laparoscopic excision of ovarian cystic lesions.

41. **Answer: A**
    59150 -- laparoscopic treatment of ectopic pregnancy, without salpingectomy and/or oophorectomy is the appropriate code for above procedure. For patient's ectopic pregnancy physician removed a fetus that is within the pelvic cavity. Provider performed this procedure using laparoscope and does not removed the fallopian tube or ovary.

42. **Answer: C**
    50544 -- laparoscopy, surgical, pyeloplasty, and 52332 cystourethroscopy, with insertion of indwelling ureteral stent are the appropriate codes for this procedure. Since patient was suffering with hydronephrosis provider corrected the blockage between the kidney and the ureter with a surgical intervention. Also, provider performed cystourethroscopy, the inspection of the interior of the bladder, the urethra, prostatic urethra, and ureteric openings using a cystoscope passed through the urethra and into the bladder, and inserts an indwelling stent into the ureter.

43. **Answer: B**
    59820 -- treatment of missed abortion, completed surgically; first trimester is the appropriate code for this procedure. Since patient is coming with missed abortion provider surgically removes the fetus and all of the products of conception. Patient's gestational age is 7 weeks, took first trimester. Provider performs this procedure via a vaginal approach to abort the fetus which has died in the uterus before birth.

44. **Answer: A**
    57250 -- posterior colporrhaphy, repair of rectocele with or without perineorrhaphy, and 57285 -- paravaginal defect repair, vaginal approach are the right codes for this procedure. Since patient is suffering from rectocele provider repaired rectum and vagina with surgical intervention.

45. **Answer: D**
    51741 -- complex uroflowmetry (e.g., calibrated electronic equipment) is the right answer for this question. Physician done complex procedure of uroflowmetry with electronic equipment to record the volume of the urine for patient's condition.

46. **Answer: C**
    56740 -- excision of Bartholin's gland or cyst is the right answer which is not required to code skin closure separately along with this code. This code includes the skin closure which will be done in layers using absorbable material.

47. **Answer: D**
    59514 -- cesarean delivery only. This procedure is not including postpartum care, routine obstetric care or antepartum care. It is a direct code with search words C-Section or cesarean delivery.

48. **Answer: A**
    For patient's complaints irregular menstruation physician performed hysteroscopy biopsy to find out the reason, which came out the endometrial hyperplasia. 58558 -- hysteroscopy, surgical; with sampling (biopsy) of endometrium and/or polypectomy, with or without D & C is the direct CPT code for this procedure.

60,000 Series

49. **Answer: A**
Since thyroid lobe removed should be code 60220 total thyroid lobectomy, unilateral, with or without isthunusectomy and should not code thyroidectomy, 31500 -- intubation, endotracheal is included in the primary procedure thyroid lobectomy. RT for Laterality used to identify procedures performed on the right side of the body.

50. **Answer: A**
63030 -- laminotomy with decompression of nerve roots, including partial facetectomy, foraminotomy and/or excision of herniated intervertebral disc; 1 interspace, lumbar is the right code for above procedure. M54.32 sciatica, left side is the ICD code for patient's complaint.

51. **Answer: C**
60300 -- aspiration and/or injection, thyroid cyst is the appropriate code for this position. Since patient is suffering with thyroid cyst, physician drained the cyst to treat thyroid cyst and sample sent to the lab to detect cancer.

52. **Answer: A**
62141 -- cranioplasty for skull defect; larger than 5 cm diameter is the appropriate code for this procedure. For patient's condition traumatic brain injury provider removed a portion of skull bone and repaired a defect in the skull that is larger than 5 cm diameter.

53. **Answer: C**
69205 -- removal foreign body from external auditory canal; with general anesthesia is the right code for this procedure. In this procedure bead is removed from the external auditory canal from the right ear. LT for Laterality used to identify procedures performed on the right side of the body.

54. **Answer: A**
61140 -- burr hole or trephine; with biopsy of brain or intracranial lesion is the right code for this procedure. Provider drilled holes into the skull to remove a small biopsy of abnormal tissue for testing. Codification done with this code as only biopsy done not draining the cyst or tapping of the cyst done.

55. **Answer: D**
65770 -- keratoprosthesis is the appropriate code for this procedure. Since patient is suffering with Keratoconus, which is a chronic condition and can degrade vision to a level

where one will experience difficulty leading normal life, physician treated with surgical intervention by placing ferrara ring implant in cornea. LT for Laterality used to identify procedures performed on the right side of the body.

56. **Answer: A**
    67930 -- suture of recent wound, eyelid, involving lid margin, tarsus, and/or palpebral conjunctiva direct closure; partial thickness is right code for this procedure. The provider closed a wound in the eyelid of recent origin. He sutured the wound edges together as a direct closure. Modifier E3 used to identify right upper eyelid.

57. **Answer: A**
    For patient's condition Injection to the intra tympanic done, which is Labyrinthectomy, with perfusion of vestibuloactive drug to transcanal. LT modifier is indicative for left ear.

58. **Answer: B**
    Physician performed 67312 -- strabismus surgery, recession or resection procedure; 2 horizontal muscles for two muscles, which are Lateral rectus and medial rectus for patients left eye exotropia. Add on code 67335 is for the placement of adjustable sutures for the primary procedure. Modifier LT is indicative of laterality of the eye.

59. **Answer: C**
    For patient's complaint exudative retinopathy right eye, physician injected pharmacologic agent into pars plana of the eye. 67028 is intravitreal drug delivery system to provide consistent delivery of a drug to an area of the eye affect by disease. This procedure is capable of releasing a controlled amount of a specific drug for months, avoiding drug toxicity and other problems associated with prolonged intravenous therapies.

60. **Answer: B**
    Physician performed thyroidectomy with radical neck dissection for patient's condition malignant neoplasm of thyroid gland. This procedure is not simple or not with limited radical dissection. It is complete radical neck dissection. 60254 -- thyroidectomy, total or subtotal for malignancy, with radical neck dissection is the right answer for this procedure.

Evaluation and Management

61. **Answer: A**
    99214 -- office or other outpatient visit for the evaluation and management of an established patient is with History-Detailed, Examination-Detailed, MDM-Moderate complexity is the appropriate code for this patient visit. Since patient is coming for follow up this visit can be considered as established patient with level 99214.

62. **Answer: B**
    99202 -- office or other outpatient visit for the evaluation and management of a new patient with History, examination of EPF and medical decision making is straight forward going to 2nd level of E&M. Since patient is a new patient for this visit can be considered 99202.

63. **Answer: D**
    99291 -- critical care, evaluation, and management of the critically ill or critically injured patient; first 30-74, and 99292 -- each additional 30 minutes are the right codes for this patient care. Since critical care services provided for 1 hour 30 minutes and the total minutes are 90 minutes which goes to 99291 and add on code 99292.

64. **Answer: C**
    99222 -- initial hospital care, per day, for the evaluation and management of a patient is the right code for comprehensive history and examination and moderate complexity of medical decision making.

65. **Answer: B**
    4 is the right answer for this question. Out of 8 HPI elements, 4 elements should be required to meet extended HPI.

66. **Answer: A**
    In emergency department there will be no distinction between new and established patients. Emergency department only defined as a hospital-based facility for the provision of unscheduled episodic services to patients who present for immediate medical attention.

67. **Answer: D**
    Emergency room evaluation and management code 99284 is A detailed history; a detailed examination; and medical decision making of moderate complexity. For emergency room E&M codes total three key components should meet where in the above service all key components are meeting for 99284.

68. **Answer: B**

    Established evaluation and management code 99214 correct code. History is going to detailed examination with all elements from HPI, ROS, and PFSH. Physical exam is going to detailed exam and medical decision making going to moderate. This all elements and key components are meeting to 99214.

69. **Answer: A**

    Initial day admission code 99221 -- initial hospital care, per day, for the evaluation and management of a patient, which requires thee key components a detailed history, a detailed or comprehensive examination and a low complexity of medical decision making.

Anesthesia

70. **Answer: A**
    01961 -- anesthesia for cesarean delivery only is the right code for this procedure. The anesthesia provider performs a pre-operative evaluation of the patient, induces the patient and monitor the patient during a cesarean delivery that a different provider performs.

71. **Answer: C**
    01830 -- anesthesia for open or surgical arthroscopic procedures on distal radius, distal ulna, wrist or hand joints is the right answer for this procedure. The anesthesia provider notes any types and amounts of medications administered, all forms of monitoring used, patient responses, and the start and stop times of anesthesia care.

72. **Answer: B**
    P3 is the physical status modifier which states "A patient with severe systemic disease." When anesthesia performed on a patient who is with sever systemic disease along with anesthesia code, we should append P3 modifier.

73. **Answer: D**
    01820 -- anesthesia for all closed procedures on radius, ulna, wrist or hand bones is the right answer for this procedure. Since closed reduction is the closed procedure of the hand bones picked this code for anesthesia services.

74. **Answer: A**
    Anesthesia on patella and tibia is 01392 -- anesthesia for all open procedures on upper ends of tibia, fibula, and/or patella. Open procedure done on this patient for his patellar fracture and internal fixation. Patient is a 71-year-old added add on code 99100 -- anesthesia for patient of extreme age, younger than one year and older than 70.

75. **Answer: C**
    Anesthesia time begins when the anesthesiologist begins to prepare the patient for the induction of anesthesia in the operating room and ends when the patient may be safely placed under postoperative supervision. For above service should count anesthesia time from 4:00 p.m. to 5:30 p.m., which comes to 1 hour 30 minutes.

Radiology

76. **Answer: B**
    73620 -- radiological examination, foot; 2 views is the right answer for this X-ray. Since patient is suffering with right foot pain physician ordered X-ray of foot two views to find the cause of the pain, which is revealed advanced degenerating changes of the foot. RT used to identify procedures performed on the right side of the body.

77. **Answer: C**
    73700 -- computed tomography, lower extremity; without contrast material is the right answer for this CT scan. In this procedure provider performed a CT scan of the patient's lower extremity without using contrast material to diagnose a disease of the lower extremity. LT used to identify procedures performed on the left side of the body.

78. **Answer: A**
    72195 -- magnetic resonance imaging, pelvis; without contrast material is the right answer for this MRI. MRI uses magnetic fields and radio waves to visualize body tissues to diagnose, manage, and treat diseases.

79. **Answer: C**
    76536 -- ultrasound, soft tissues of head and neck, real time with imaging documentation is the right answer for this US scan. Provider performed real time ultrasound examination of the soft tissues of the neck and records and saved the image for the review.

80. **Answer: B**
    71250 -- computed tomography, thorax; without contrast material is the right answer for this case. Provider performed a computed tomography examination of the thorax without using contrast material diagnose and treat disease. Since patient is coming with COVID infection physician performed this CT to analyze the infection of the chest.

81. **Answer: D**
    73721 -- magnetic resonance imaging, any joint of lower extremity; without contrast material is the right answer for this procedure. Provider performed magnetic resonance imaging of a lower extremity joint without using contrast material. The technician captures the radiofrequency signals generated by the body and the computer generates a series of imaging that display slices of the leg, focusing on a specific joint. RT used to identify procedures performed on the right side of the body.

82. **Answer: A**
X-Ray performed on spine, lumbosacral region with two views, which are AP and lateral views, coded 72100 -- radiologic examination, spine, lumbosacral; 2 or 3 views. For the code 72100 includes minimum of 2 views.

83. **Answer: C**
This is complete ultrasound of the abdomen is evaluation of the abdominal organs of all 8 anatomic regions, which are liver, spleen, gallbladder, common bile duct, pancreas, kidneys, abdominal aorta and IVC.

84. **Answer: A**
As patient is coming for routine ultrasound for left breast physician performed 76645 -- ultrasound breast(s), real time with image documentation, with results of benign mass N63.20 unspecified lump in the left breast, unspecified quadrant.

Laboratory/Pathology

85. **Answer: B**
    85610 -- prothrombin time is measured using the blood plasma. This is to analyze if a blood thinner agent or anticoagulant drug, which is coumadin is working, the drug is mixed in blood plasma or the patient is instructed to take the medicine before the test.

86. **Answer: D**
    The lab analyst measures the iron level 83540 to check hemoglobin levels in the blood. Analyst performs the technical steps to quantitate the iron level which accurately measures the amount of the chemical element iron is present in hemoglobin and is an essential element needed in the body.

87. **Answer: C**
    85025 -- blood count; complete (CBC), automated (Hgb, Hct, RBC, WBC and platelets count) and automated differential WBC count is the right answer for this lab test. This blood test provides detailed information about various types of cells in a patient's blood. Counting, measuring and analyzing blood cells are part of this procedure code.

88. **Answer: A**
    83690 -- lipase done to test to measure the amount of lipase enzyme in the patient specimen. Provider ordered this test to evaluate patient's abnormal levels of lipase enzymes, which will cause abdominal pain. Treatment will be provided depending upon the levels of the lipase enzymes.

89. **Answer: B**
    82306 -- Vitamin D; 25 hydroxy, includes fraction(s), if performed is the answer for this lab test. It measures the vitamin D level. The analysis measures the major circulating form of vitamin D that helps regulate calcium and phosphorus. Physician ordered for Vitamin D to diagnose and treat vitamin D deficiency.

90. **Answer: D**
    Renal function panel is included carbon dioxide, potassium and albumin, but not included Igm antibody in its panel. Renal function panel test is to measure the blood level of certain chemicals including albumin, blood urea nitrogen, total calcium, carbon dioxide, chloride, creatinine, glucose, phosphorus inorganic, potassium and sodium. Igm antibody is not in the renal function panel to measure.

91. **Answer: B**
    This panel is BMP total, which includes all calcium, CO2, chloride, creatinine, glucose, potassium, sodium and BUN. All the labs performed, and results discussed. 80048 coded as this panel code is correct code for above laboratory services.

92. **Answer: D**
    For patient's complaints and symptoms physician performed Thyroid Stimulating Hormone to determine thyroid function to differentiate from various types of hypothyroidism. 84443 is the right code for this service provided by the physician.

93. **Answer: C**
    As this panel is not completely done with all labs, should not code the panel code. This lab tests should be divided and code whatever labs done. 82040 -- albumin; serum, plasma or whole blood, 82247 -- bilirubin total, 82248 -- bilirubin direct, 84075 -- phosphatase alkaline and 84155 -- protein, total, except by refractometry; serum, plasma or whole blood.

Medicine

94. **Answer: D**

    93971 -- duplex scan of extremity veins including responses to compression and other maneuvers; unilateral or limited study is the right answer for above venous Doppler study. Physician can visualize and selectively assess the flow patterns of peripheral vessels using real time ultrasound imaging and pulsed Doppler. LT used to identify procedures performed on the left side of the body.

95. **Answer: B**

    96360 -- intravenous infusion, hydration; initial, 31 minutes to 1 hour and 96361 intravenous infusion, hydration; each additional hour is the right answer for this hydration service. Initial code 96360 should come always as a primary code and the add on code 96361 -- following to primary code. Since normal saline administered for 2 hours this two codes 96360 for the 1st hour and 96361 for the 2nd hour should be coded for this service.

96. **Answer: D**

    96413 -- chemotherapy administration, intravenous infusion technique; up to 1 hour, single or initial substance/drug is the right answer for this service. Chemotherapy is a therapeutic procedure used for the treatment of the cancer via the use of chemical agents. In this service physician administers the chemotherapy drugs intravenously as a single dose and the infusion may continue up to a maximum time of one hour.

97. **Answer: C**

    95905 -- motor and sensory nerve conduction, using preconfigured electrode array(s), amplitude and latency/velocity study, each limb, included F-wave study when performed is the right answer for this test. These are diagnostic tests to evaluate the function, especially the ability of electric conduction, of the motor and sensory nerves of the human body.

98. **Answer: A**

    94002 -- ventilation assist and management, initiation of pressure or volume preset ventilators for assisted or controlled breathing; hospital inpatient/observation, initial day is the right answer for this service. This code is for the initial setting of ventilator parameters for the patient where he cannot breathe on his own. The service is performed for a hospital inpatient first day of treatment.

99. **Answer: D**

    90460 -- immunization administration through 18 years of age via any route of administration, with counseling by physician or other qualified health care professional;

first or only component of each vaccine or toxoid administered is the right answer for this vaccination service. The provider administers a single live vaccine through a any route to a patient up to 18 years of age.

100. **Answer: D**
As per the hierarchy infusion-push-hydration should be coded. 96365 -- intravenous infusion, for therapy, prophylaxis or diagnosis; initial, up to 1 hour is the first code for the drug Viasol 40mg administered for 1 hour. For Zofran which is administered as push coded with add on code 96375 -- therapeutic, prophylactic, or diagnostic injection; each additional sequential intravenous push of a new substance/drug. Ringer lactate which is administered for one hour is coded with add on code 96361 -- intravenous infusion, hydration; each additional hour.

101. **Answer: B**
As patient is coming for hemodialysis and rendered the service coded 90935 -- hemodialysis procedure with single evaluation by a physician or other health care qualified professional. Evaluation and Management services are included in 90935, should not code physician services separately.

102. **Answer: D**
As per the performed procedure 95816 is the correct answer which is Electroencephalogram (EEG); including recording awake and drowsy. This service provided to the patient in wakefulness and drowsiness for the complaints of generalized tonic-clonic seizure.

Medical Terminology

103. **Answer: C**
Biopsy is the terminology for the removal of a portion or the entirety of suspicious tissue for pathologic examination. The provider performs the procedure as an investigation or treatment for that particular suspicious tissue.

104. **Answer: A**
Hemostasis is a natural process of blood clot formation or stoppage of blood flow at the site of injury. When a blood vessel wall is disrupted, the hemostatic response will be quick, localized and carefully regulated. Abnormal bleeding or thrombosis may occur when specific elements of these processes are missing.

105. **Answer: D**
Posterior describes the back of the body. Example is the heart is posterior to the sternum because it lies behind the sternum. Posterior defines something that is situated at the back of something else.

106. **Answer: A**
Oxygen is measurement of the level of oxygen in the blood. By using a small device called a pulse oximetry, blood oxygen level can be checked without to be stuck with a needle, which is a percentage of the blood is carrying oxygen.

107. **Answer: C**
Prosthesis is an artificial device that replaces a body part, which is a missing or impaired body part. Prostheses are manmade substitutes for body parts that have been damaged or removed from trauma, disease or any other cause.

108. **Answer: A**
Retractor is a surgical instrument used to separate edges of a surgical wound or incision, or to hold back underlying organs and tissues so that body parts under the incision may be accessed. It helps surgeons and operating room professionals during the surgical procedures to give better visualization and access to the performing surgery.

109. **Answer: C**
Prefix eu- is good, well or normal. Examples are Eupepsia-good digestion, euphoria-a state of intense excitement and happiness and eupnea-normal and good breathing.

110. **Answer: A**

Patient will be placed on prone position, which means patient will be placed face down position or palm down position for few radiological imaging or few procedures.

111. **Answer: D**

In medical terminology Hex- means Six. Examples are Hexapartite, which means six parts. Hexose, which means six carbon atoms in chemistry.

Anatomy

112. **Answer: B**
Lateral compartment is one of the three joint compartments in the knee, formed by the outer knuckle of the femur, or thigh bone, where it attaches to the tibia bone in the lower leg. It also called the peroneal compartment, is made up of two muscles, which are peroneus longus and peroneus brevis. The common function of the muscles is eversion-turning the sole of the foot outwards.

113. **Answer: C**
The cornea is the transparent part of the eyeball that covers the front portion of the eyeball. It also covers the pupil, iris and anterior chamber. The cornea's main function is eye to focus light to see clearly. It allows light to enter the eye.

114. **Answer: A**
Bile is a substance produced in the liver a greenish yellow secretion which will passed to the gallbladder for concentration, storage or transport into the first region of the small intestines, the duodenum. Its function is to aid in the digestion of fats in the duodenum. Bile is composed of bile acids and salts, phospholipids, cholesterol, pigments, water and electrolyte chemicals.

115. **Answer: D**
Intestine is the digestive tract from the pylorus, the opening at the bottom of the stomach all the way the anus. It's a muscular tube, which is long continuous tube running from the stomach to the anus. Intestines include the small intestine, large intestine and rectum.

116. **Answer: A**
The scrotum is the sac that contains the testes or testicles, which is like a pouch made up of skin. It is a part of the external male genitalia located behind and underneath the penis. It's a small muscular sac which protects the testicles, blood vessels, and part of the spermatic cord.

117. **Answer: D**
Humerus is the bone in the upper arm that runs from the shoulder to the elbow. The humerus is the long bone of the upper extremity of the human body. It consists of a proximal end, a shaft and a distal end all which contain important anatomical landmarks.

118. **Answer: A**

Epidermis, dermis and subcutaneous tissue are the right answer. The epidermis, the outermost layer of the skin, provides a waterproof barrier and creates our skin tone. The dermis, beneath the epidermis, contains connective tissue, hair follicles and sweat glands. The deeper layer is subcutaneous tissue is made of fat and connective tissue.

119. **Answer: B**

The spinal cord is located in the vertebral foramen and is made up of 31 segments: 8 cervical, 12 thoracic, 5 lumbar, 5 sacral and 1 coccygeal.

120. **Answer: C**

The uterine artery is a branch of the anterior division of the internal iliac artery that provides blood supply to the uterus among other productive organs in female.

ICD-10-CM/Diagnosis

121. **Answer: D**
K35.80 Unspecified acute appendicitis is the right answer for this patient case. A disorder characterized by acute inflammation to the vermiform appendix caused by a pathogenic agent. Immediate removal of appendix is required to avoid rupture of the appendix, which is life threaten to the patient.

122. **Answer: B**
D17.0 Benign lipomatous neoplasm of skin and subcutaneous tissue of head, face and neck is the right answer for this patient's condition. A benign lipoma, which appears as a soft, lobular, painful, noncancerous mass covered by a thin, fibrous capsule. It occurs below the surface of the skin due to multiplication of white adipocytes, which are fat cells.

123. **Answer: A**
M67.431 ganglion, right wrist is the right answer for this patient's condition. Ganglion of the right wrist refers to a generally harmless soft tissue mass filled with a thick fluid that forms under the skin near a wrist joint or tendon. Surgical intervention is required for this patient since patient is having chronic pain and it is increasing with his daily activities.

124. **Answer: D**
D18.02 hemangioma of intracranial structures is the right answer for this case. Hemangioma of structures within the skull refers to a benign growth that results from abnormal multiplication of blood vessels in the brain and meninges.

125. **Answer: A**
N11.1 chronic obstructive pyelonephritis is the right answer for this patient's case. This is characterized by renal inflammation and scarring induced by recurrent or persistent renal infection.

126. **Answer: C**
A54.24 Gonococcal female pelvic inflammatory disease is the right answer for this diagnosis. This is refers to manifestations of a venereal disease which affects the reproductive organs in the pelvic cavity and the membranes that covers them, it is caused by the bacterium Neisseria gonorrhoeae, transmitted sexually.

127. **Answer: B**

K81.0 acute cholecystitis is the right answer. Acute cholecystitis is an inflammation of the gallbladder occurs due to a gallstone getting stuck in the opening. It is a potentially serious condition that usually needs to treat surgically.

128. **Answer: D**

C61 malignant neoplasm of prostate and R97.21 rising PSA following treatment for malignant neoplasm of prostate is the right answer for this case. Since patient has elevated PSA, R97.21 should be coded along with C61. Patients with malignant neoplasm of the prostate will have painful urination, prostate enlargement, blood in the urine and so on. Depending on the stage of the cancer, treatment involves chemotherapy, radiation therapy, surgical excision of tumors or radical prostatectomy.

129. **Answer: A**

As patient is coming for chemotherapy, Primary code would be Z51.11 encounter for antineoplastic chemotherapy. Secondary code would be C50.111 Malignant neoplasm of central portion of right female breast. Patient also has hypothyroidism, coded E03.9.

130. **Answer: D**

Patient has CKD-4 with HTN and diabetes mellitus. HTN with CKD-4 is hypertensive chronic kidney disease with stage 1 through stage 4 chronic kidney disease, or unspecified chronic kidney disease and diabetes with CKD-4 is Type 2 diabetes mellitus with diabetic chronic kidney disease.

131. **Answer: A**

As patient is having gestational diabetes in pregnancy which is controlled by insulin is coded with O24.414. Weeks of gestation coded with Z3A.34 as patient is 34 weeks pregnant and Z79.4 is for long term (current) use of Insulin.

132. **Answer: C**

As patient is diagnosed with right knee tear of posterior horn of medial meniscus with old injury is coded with M23.221 and tear of posterior horn of lateral meniscus with old injury is coded with M23.251. Symptoms pain and swelling should not be code as definitive diagnosis is present for this patient.

HCPCS Level II

133. **Answer: A**
J7510 is the HCPCS Level II code for Prednisolone, oral, 5 mg. Prednisolone works in the body of a patient to prevent the release of inflammation causing substances. A provider reports this code for each 5 mg of prednisolone. The route of administration includes oral administration.

134. **Answer: C**
This code covers the supply of an implantable access system for use as a dialysis port in patient undergoing long term dialysis. When the patient requires dialysis, the provider inserts a needle through the port to access the vascular system rather than having to insert a needle in the patient's vein each time.

135. **Answer: B**
The code Q0081 -- infusion therapy, using other than chemotherapeutic drugs, per visit reports infusion therapy, which is the administration of medication through indwelling intravenous line, subcutaneous catheter, or port. This code does not include medications given for chemotherapy.

136. **Answer: A**
A0429 -- ambulance service, basic life support, emergency transport is the right answer for this service. This code represents the emergency transport by the ambulance staff including the necessary supplies and services. Basic life support ambulance transport provides transport for a patient to travel one location to another due to medical condition. The ambulance staffs are qualified emergency professional and the ambulance has specialized instruments.

137. **Answer: B**
As patient was applied with thumb spica splint, which will support the CMC joint and immobilize the MCP joint of the thumb without inhibiting hand movement. L3807 is wrist hand finger orthosis, without joint(s), prefabricated item that has been trimmed, bent, molded, assembled, or otherwise customized to fit a specific patient by an individual with expertise is the correct HCPCS code for above service. HCPCS level II modifier F5 indicates anatomical site, where the splint applied.

138. **Answer: A**
L8030 is breast prosthesis; silicone or equal, without integral adhesive is right answer. HCPCS level II code L8030 is the code for this service as patient was implanted with silicone material for her breast implantation. RT is to indicate the laterality of the procedure.

Coding guidelines

139. **Answer: B**

    As per coding convention from official coding guidelines the word "And" should be interpreted to mean either "and" or "or" when it appears in a title. For example, can read and as "and" or "or" in code G02 Meningitis in other infectious and parasitic diseases classified elsewhere for the word "and."

140. **Answer: B**

    As per official coding guidelines codes that describe signs and symptoms are acceptable for reporting purposes when a related definitive diagnosis has not been established or confirmed by the provider.

141. **Answer: D**

    Sequence Acute code first following chronic code If the same condition is described as both acute and chronic and separate subentries are existing in the Alphabetic index at the same indentation level. Should code both codes sequencing Acute code first.

142. **Answer: A**

    E11.9 Type II diabetes without complications is the right answer when the type of diabetes is not documented in the medical record. E11.9 is the default code when diabetes type is not mentioned by the provider.

143. **Answer: D**

    The postpartum period begins immediately and continues till six weeks following delivery. A postpartum complication is any complication occurring within six-week period.

144. **Answer: B**

    As per official coding guidelines if no bilateral code is provided and the condition is bilateral, assign separates codes for both the left and right side. Example: Patient is suffering with right knee and left knee pain is needed to code both sides separately with M25.562 and M25.561, because bilateral code is not provided.

Compliance and Regulatory

145. **Answer: C**

    CPT is a descriptive of terms and identifying codes for reporting medical services and procedures with the purpose to provide uniform language among physicians, patients and third parties. That will accurately describe medical, surgical, and diagnostic services and will thereby provide an effective means for reliable nationwide communication between physicians, other qualified healthcare professionals, patients and third parties.

146. **Answer: A**

    Non face-to-face services, telephonic and online services are valid coding services. The codes are used to report episodes of the patient care.

147. **Answer: B**

    The CPT code set is published annually as both electronic data files and books and is effective date for the use of the updated CPT code set is January 1st of every year. Changes to the CPT code set are mean to be applied prospectively from the effective date.

148. **Answer: B**

    It is recognized that there may be services or procedures performed by physicians or other qualified health care professionals that are not found in the CPT code set. Therefore, a number of specific code numbers have been designated for reporting unlisted procedures. CPT will allow to code unlisted procedure codes for the services, which are not found in the CPT code set.

149. **Answer: C**

    CPT code set is under Health Insurance Portability and Accountability Act (HIPAA). This means that for all financial and administrative health care transactions sent electronically, the CPT code set will need to be used.

150. **Answer: A**

    It is correct that add-on codes are always performed in addition to the primary service or procedure and must never be reported as a stand-alone code.